In ~

THE JEWS OF MOSCOW, KIEV AND MINSK

The Jews of Moscow, Kiev and Minsk

Identity, Antisemitism, Emigration

Robert J. Brym
*Professor, Department of Sociology
and Centre for Russian and East European Studies
University of Toronto*

with the assistance of

Rozalina Ryvkina
*Professor
All-Russian Centre for Public Opinion
Research, Moscow*

Editor
Howard Spier
*Head of Central and East European Department
Institute of Jewish Affairs
London*

MACMILLAN

in association with the
Institute of Jewish Affairs

For Rhonda, Shira, Talia and Ariella

First published 1994 by
THE MACMILLAN PRESS LTD
Houndmills, Basingstoke, Hampshire RG21 2XS
and London
Companies and representatives
throughout the world

in association with the
Institute of Jewish Affairs
79 Wimpole Street
London WIM 7DD
Great Britain

ISBN 0–333–61752–5

A catalogue record for this book is available
from the British Library.

Printed in Great Britain by
Mackays of Chatham PLC
Chatham, Kent
Great Britain

Table of Contents

List of Tables

List of Figures

List of Photographs

Foreword

It is indisputable that in the republics which comprise the former Soviet Union Jewish culture and Judaism are undergoing an unprecedented renaissance, Jews are free to pursue virtually any career they wish, links with world Jewry and Israel proceed without obstacle and, to all intents and purposes, emigration is free. It must be emphasized that these are great and historic gains for the Jews of the former Soviet Union, for Israel and for the Jewish people as a whole.

At the same time, the fact that there is a considerable downside to this felicitous situation cannot be ignored. The shift towards a Western-style market economy in the republics of the former Soviet Union (as well as in Moscow's former satellite countries) has, as is well known, been accompanied by enormous difficulties. Most prominently perhaps in Russia and Ukraine, large sections of the population have been demoralized by an economy verging on hyper-inflation and falling living standards, social divisions have widened, and crime has grown inexorably. In addition, many Russians are deeply alarmed at their country's declining international status.

From a specifically Jewish point of view, the state-backed anti-Zionist campaign of the Brezhnev period, with its antisemitic excesses, has been replaced, in Russia, by a considerable grass-roots antisemitic movement mainly, but not entirely, on the fringe of society.

Given the grave instability experienced by Russia combined with its long tradition of authoritarianism, there are those who believe that the best the country can hope for in the medium and long term is some sort of benevolent autocracy. At the time of writing—on the occasion of Russia's first fully free parliamentary elections and a referendum on President Yeltsin's draft constitution—it has become clear that the far-right Liberal Democratic Party of Vladimir Zhirinovsky will play a substantial role in the new parliament. There can be no clearer illustration of the volatility of life in the CIS which Professor Brym rightly underlines.

As Professor Brym points out, this is "the first book based on an *in situ* survey of a representative sample of Jews in the Commonwealth of Independent States". The survey in question was conducted in the three

Slavic republics—Russia, Ukraine and Belarus—between February and April 1993. Professor Brym is also at pains to place the results of the survey in their social and historical context. Just a few short years ago the very idea of conducting a survey in these republics was unthinkable—like so much else in the countries of the post-Communist Soviet Union. Nevertheless, while the means the author employs to reach his conclusions may be novel, it is legitimate to enquire whether his findings tell us much we did not already know.

I must confess that I, and perhaps many others, have certain reservations about the value of surveys of this type. For example, do they really represent more than a snap-shot of what someone happens to be thinking at a specific moment and in certain circumstances and do respondents always give a frank answer? Also I have reservations about "sociological jargon". Having said that, I find it difficult not to be impressed by Brym's methods and the conclusions he reaches.

In the following pages Brym himself alludes to scepticism of this type. It must be said, however, that he is scrupulous in steering as clear as he possibly can of what he himself has described as "sociologese". Not only is there a refreshing absence of "jargon" in the book but Brym's language could not be less tendentious. The fairly large number of tables and charts inevitable in a work of this nature also have been reduced to the greatest possible simplicity.

The fundamental questions Brym asks in this work are the following: Precisely how many Jews are we talking about? What is the extent of their Jewishness? What factors account for variations in strength of Jewishness? How serious do they perceive the threat of antisemitism to be? How many of them are likely to emigrate and how many are likely to remain? Where are those emigrating likely to go?

Professor Brym and Professor Ryvkina asked some very valid questions and some of the results they have come up with are extremely interesting, even intriguing. To my mind, the single most important contribution to our knowledge of Jews in the three Slavonic republics—where the Jewish population of the former Soviet Union mainly resides—are the figures Brym puts forward in connection with the long disputed question of the actual size of the Jewish population. As of the beginning of 1993 there were 1,144,000 Jews in the former USSR, of whom 435,000 were in Russia, 389,000 in Ukraine, and 92,000 in Belarus, a total of approximately 916,000 (roughly 139,000 in Moscow, 85,000 in Kiev, and 31,000 in Minsk). Brym's method of calculation seems to me utterly convincing. Moreover, he completely discounts wishful thinking as well as the opinions of those who, he tells us, have a vested interest in exaggerating or playing down the figures. One suspects that the figures he comes up with are the most precise which can be attained at the present time.

On several of the other matters investigated, many of them a matter of sharp dispute between CIS-watchers, Brym sheds considerable light. On the issue of Jewish identity, for example, only about a third of Brym's respondents said they wished to be involved in the Jewish community. Similarly, on the subject of antisemitism, over 70 per cent of his respondents expressed fear of anti-Jewish activities.

In regard to the process of emigration, Brym does not hesitate to make prognostications for the future—as he himself acknowledges, a highly risky endeavour given the uncertainty which surrounds the future of these republics. Thus Brym's extremely rough projections suggest that from 1994 to 1999 just over 480,000 Jews will emigrate from the former USSR. Of these between 204,000 and 275,000 will go to Israel, and between 276,000 and 368,000 will go elsewhere. Brym also estimates that in the year 2000 less than half a million Jews will remain in the territory of the former USSR and those who do remain will for the most part be old, highly assimilated and swifly diminishing in number.

These are important conclusions which need to be taken seriously. In addition to the academic interest such research entails, there is also of course important material here for those who make policy in such matters—not only in relation to the likely numbers of emigrants, their characterization and their possible destinations but also—and not not least important—those who are likely to remain indefinitely where they are. It is very much to be hoped that attention will be paid by such persons to the results achieved by the painstaking research and dispassionate analysis demonstrated in this book.

Howard Spier

Preface

During a trip to Moscow in 1989 I was struck by an outlandish idea: might it be possible to conduct a public opinion survey in the USSR? At first I was sceptical. I needed to find competent collaborators in Moscow, establish reliable lines of communication with them and convince funders that a public opinion survey could be executed in the Soviet Union and yield meaningful results. For two years I failed on all three fronts. Then, in 1991, as the Soviet Union disintegrated, things began to fall into place for me.

These apparently contradictory events were connected. The disintegrating Soviet Union allowed more travel abroad for its academics, more involvement in international professional organizations, more exposure to Western scientific and humanistic literature—and the complement for Western academics. As a result of these sorts of contacts I met some Russian social scientists of the first rank—Dr Nikolai Popov of the All-Russian Centre for Research on Public Opinion (VTsIOM) in Moscow, Dr Andrei Degtyarev of the Department of Political Science and Sociology of Politics at Moscow State University, Professor Vladimir Yadov of the Institute of Sociology of the Russian Academy of Sciences, and Professor Rozalina Ryvkina of VTsIOM.

Professor Iadov and Dr Popov supplied me with reports on current survey research in the former USSR that I have used profitably in preparing this book. I conducted my first modest survey in Russia with Dr Degtyarev in October 1992. Some of the results of that survey were published in *Slavic Review* in 1993 and are reprinted in Chapter Four with the permission of the American Association for the Advancement of Slavic Studies. After Professor Ryvkina and I had established a collegial relationship I wrote an Introduction to a report on the refugee crisis in Russia by her and Rostislav Turovskiy. Part of that Introduction is reprinted in Chapter 2 with the permission of York Lanes Press, York University, Toronto. Most of this book, however, is based on a survey conducted with the assistance of Professor Ryvkina between February and April 1993. By means of personal visits, fax machines and electronic mail I have kept in very close touch—indeed, nearly daily contact—with Professor Ryvkina and my other collaborators for eighteen months. It has been an extraordinarily exciting experience both intellectually and personally. I am deeply indebted to my collaborators, and most especially of course to Professor Ryvkina. She has worked with diligence, efficiency and creativity to overcome what at times seemed insurmountable problems.

In Canada, Professor Robert E. Johnson, Director of the Centre for Russian and East European Studies at the University of Toronto, helped the progress of my research immeasurably by generously subsidizing my visit to Moscow and the visits of Professor Ryvkina, Dr Popov and Dr Degtyarev to Toronto. I am also extremely grateful to the Social Sciences and Humanities Research Council of Canada, which supplied the bulk of the funding for this project, and to the Humanities and Social Sciences Committee of the University of Toronto for supplementary financial assistance.

From London, Dr Howard Spier of the Institute of Jewish Affairs gave me encouragement and bibliographic help. With a firm but always friendly editor's hand, he made a number of useful suggestions for improving the manuscript.

I also wish to express my thanks to three Israeli friends—Professor Baruch Kimmerling and Professor Michael Shalev of the Department of Sociology and Social Anthropology at the Hebrew University of Jerusalem and Professor Ephraim Tabory of the Department of Sociology at Bar-Ilan University. Professors Kimmerling and Shalev provided instant and invaluable bibliographic assistance and Professor Tabory made some good suggestions for improving the questionnaire.

It is with much sadness that I must recall the support and advice which my friend, the late Professor Sidney Heitman of Colorado State University, gave me in the early stages of this project. This book is less than it could have been because it was written without the benefit of Sid's criticisms.

Most authors seem to be afflicted with stoic family members who gladly allow them to spend endless hours buried away in isolated thought. I suffer no such misfortune. My wife and three children have done their utmost to ensure that I understand clearly what is more important and what is less important in life. My debt to them is without limit. I dedicate this book to them as a symbol of my thanks and love.

RJB
Toronto, August 1993

1 The Scope of the Study

The Jews of the former Soviet Union have frequently been the subject of intense controversy. Especially during the past two-and-a-half decades, a period which may be said to have begun with the Six Day War in the Middle East, they have provoked unprecedented attention. How many of them are there? How strongly do they identify themselves as Jews? How do their patterns of identification, belief and practice vary from one category of the population to the next? Will they leave or will they stay? If they leave, where will they go? What types of Jews are most likely to emigrate? How do they perceive antisemitism in their countries? Will they be persecuted or will they enjoy new freedoms? If the latter, will they undergo a cultural revival undreamed of under Communism or will they assimilate and cease to exist as a community? These are among the chief questions that have enlivened discussions of Jews in the republics now known as the Commonwealth of Independent States. They are the questions I examine here. They have sparked debate for intellectual reasons and because they have serious policy implications not only for the CIS countries but also for Israel, the United States and some other countries such as Germany.

Too little fact has informed this debate. Expectations have therefore been dashed more than once. In 1984 it seemed to many analysts that the emigration of Soviet Jews was at an end for the foreseeable future. Yet by 1989 the rate of emigration had reached an unprecedented level. In 1989 many people expected a million Soviet Jews to emigrate to Israel in the next three years. In the event, 39 per cent of that number arrived. In 1990 pogroms were expected by some circles in Russia. None materialized. Unforeseen, singular events—the rise of Gorbachev, the collapse of Communism, the Gulf War—obviously played a large part in confounding people's expectations. The surprises might not have been so great, however, if analysts had been less emboldened by ideological certainty and better able to survey the actual intentions, perceptions, motivations and fears of Jews in the region as well as the degree to which they were rooted in their social circumstances.

Until very recently, such surveys were out of the question. Freedom

1

to conduct surveys of public opinion in the Soviet Union dates only from the late 1980s. Local expertise was also lacking. Tatyana Zaslavskaya, one of the top sociologists in the former Soviet Union and an advisor to Gorbachev, remarked in *Pravda* in 1987 that "Soviet sociology is sociology without sociologists."[1] Nor could Western sociologists immediately hope to undertake surveys themselves. The terrain was unknown and the pitfalls many. Finally, most of the Western individuals and organizations that could have funded survey research on Soviet Jews were justifiably sceptical of its success.[2]

All this is now beginning to change, as this book testifies. The main survey on which this book is based was funded by a grant from the Social Sciences and Humanities Research Council of Canada.[3] Professor Ryvkina and I designed the questionnaire with the assistance of Dr Leonid Kosals of VTsIOM. Professor Ryvkina designed the sample and organized the field work. She was assisted by Dr Leonid Kosals and she consulted with Professor A. V. Superanskaya. I analyzed the data and wrote the book, taking into account Professor Ryvkina's critical comments on the first draft. The result of this effort is the first book based on an *in situ* survey of a representative sample of Jews in the Commonwealth of Independent States (CIS).

Due to financial considerations I had to limit the survey to the Jews of Moscow, Kiev and Minsk, the capital cities of Russia, Ukraine and Belarus respectively. The Jews in those three cities account for approximately 28 per cent of all Jews residing in the three Slavic republics of the CIS (see Table 1.1). I strongly suspect that my findings are generalizable to all Jews living in the larger cities of the three republics but I cannot test my suspicion until I conduct more extensive sampling at some future date. I am, however, confident that within known limits my findings are generalizable to the Jews of the three capital cities because of the way the sample was selected.

In the autumn of 1992 Professor Ryvkina contacted Professor A. V. Superanskaya, a leading linguist in Moscow who specializes in the study of Jewish surnames. Professor Superanskaya drew up a list of the 405 most common Jewish surnames in Russia, Ukraine and Belarus (see Appendix A). The list was given to the police offices in Moscow, Kiev and Minsk which are responsible for keeping computerized records of all city residents. The head of the police office in each city was paid to have his computer generate at random a list of 1,110 households with family surnames corresponding to those on the list of 405.

Dr Kosals then selected every third household from each of the police lists—334 from Moscow and 333 from each of Kiev and Minsk. An

Table 1.1
Jewish Census Population (1989) and Sample Size

	Russia	Ukraine	Belarus	Total
population	550,000	487,000	112,000	1,149,000
% of total Jews	48	42	10	100

	Moscow	Kiev	Minsk	total
est. population	175,500	107,000	39,500	322,000
% of republic Jews	32	22	35	28
% of Jews in 3 cities	54	33	12	100
actual interviews	334	333	333	1,000
weighted interviews	545	332	123	1,000
weighting factor	1.63	1.00	0.37	—

Source for republic population data: Sidney Heitman, "Jews in the 1989 USSR census", *Soviet Jewish Affairs*, vol. 20, no.1, 1990, 23-30.

alternative list of the remaining addresses was also compiled. If, after three attempts, it was not possible to interview anyone in a household from the first list, a household from the alternative list was selected at random.

Interviewing was conducted between 3 February and 17 April 1993 by 102 trained interviewers, sixty-one of whom were Jewish. If only one adult was at home the interviewer tried to interview that person. If more than one adult was at home the interviewer asked to interview the person in the household who was eighteen years of age or older and had had the most recent birthday. That was done in order to randomize the selection of individuals within households. If it was not possible to interview the selected person at the time of initial contact or at some future date the interviewer obtained some minimal information about the selected person's social characteristics and drew a new household from the alternative list. This procedure was repeated if necessary.[4]

The interviewers continued in this way until 1,000 Jews had been interviewed in the three cities. A total of 1,207 actual contacts were made to obtain the 1,000 interviews; 207 contacts refused to participate in the study. Thus the response rate was a very high 83 per cent. Because of the randomization procedures followed, I am confident that the 1,000 respondents are representative of the Jewish populations of Moscow, Kiev and Minsk.[5]

The questionnaire is reproduced in Appendix B. It consists of 157 questions that were answered by respondents and twenty-three questions that were answered by interviewers. The interviews were conducted on a face-to-face basis in the respondents' homes, about half of them beginning between 5:00 pm and 8:00 pm and the other half scattered throughout the day. The interviews lasted anywhere from 10 to 120 minutes, depending on how many questions were answered and on how much time was required to explain questions to respondents. Over two-thirds of the interviews took between 30 and 60 minutes. On average, each interview lasted 36 minutes.

As can be seen in Table 1.1, Moscow Jews constitute about 54 per cent of Jews in the three cities, Kiev Jews about 33 per cent and Minsk Jews the remaining 12 per cent. In order to draw accurate inferences about the Jewish populations of the three cities as a whole I was obliged to weight the replies given by respondents to take account of that distribution. Thus each Moscow interview was "counted" 1.63 times, each Kiev interview once, and each Minsk interview 0.37 times.

One can be confident that the results reported below are accurate plus or minus 3.1 per cent at the 95 per cent confidence level. This means that if one were to draw twenty random samples of 1,000 people each, and report results from each of those twenty samples, nineteen of them would be at most within 3.1 per cent of the results I report.

In order to appreciate fully the significance of the survey results it is necessary to place them in social and historical context. The following chapter provides that background as briefly as possible. Because of the survey's topicality, and in the interest of getting the survey results published while they are still fresh, I decided not to take the time to paint an elaborate socio-historical portrait. Instead the following chapter draws a sketch that accentuates only two issues. I first explain why ethnic distinctiveness persisted and even became accentuated in the Soviet era. I then describe the position of Jews in Soviet and post-Soviet society and some of the dilemmas they face.

NOTES

1   Tatyana Zaslavskaya, "*Perestroyka* and sociology", *Pravda*, 6 February 1987. See also Rozalina Ryvkina, "From civic courage to scientific demonstration", *Soviet Sociology*, vol. 28, no. 5, 1989, 7-23; Robert J. Brym, "Sociology, *perestroika*, and Soviet society", *Canadian Journal of Sociology*, vol. 15, no. 2, 1990, 207-15.

2   The only exception of which I am aware is the American Jewish Committee, which has funded research on antisemitism since 1989. See Lev D. Gudkov and Alex G. Levinson, *Attitudes Toward Jews in the Soviet Union: Public Opinion in Ten Republics* (New York: American Jewish Committee, 1992); L. Gudkov and A. Levinson, "Attitudes towards Jews", *Sotsiologicheskiye issledovaniya*, no. 12, 1992, 108-11; James L. Gibson and Raymond M. Duch, "Anti-semitic attitudes of the mass public: Estimates and explanations based on a survey of the Moscow oblast", *Public Opinion Quarterly*, vol. 56, 1992, 1-28. For a good up-to-date synopsis of problems of survey research in the CIS see Michael Swafford, "Sociological aspects of survey research in the Commonwealth of Independent States", *International Journal of Public Opinion Research*, vol. 4, no. 4, 1992, 346-57.

3   In addition, I will refer to the results of a telephone poll of 946 non-Jewish adult Muscovites which I conducted in October 1992 with the assistance of Professor Andrei Degtyarev of Moscow State University. For methodological details see Chapter 4.

4   Nearly three-quarters of interviews were conducted on the first try, nearly 11 per cent on the second, and just over 8 per cent on the third. In order to verify that interviews were being conducted as reported, administrators at the branches of the All-Russian Centre for Public Opinion Research (VTsIOM) in each city made random telephone checks on just over 12 per cent of the respondents.

5   Jews by any criterion who Slavicized their surnames are not found either in our sample or in the 1993 population estimates given in Chapter 3. Are they Jews? Consider the following anecdote, related by Aleksandr Burakovsky, Chairman of the Kiev Sholem Aleichem Society, in 1992. Burakovsky relates that during business trips to the Russian city of Chelyabinsk, where many Ukrainian Jews fled the Nazis, "I see young men with Jewish features, and I ask them, and their names are Ivanov and Petrov, good Russian names. And I ask them about their parents and their grandparents, and they're all Ukrainian." See Steven Erlanger, "As Ukraine loses Jews, the Jews lose a tradition", *The New York Times*, 27 August 1992.

2 The Jews in Soviet and Post-Soviet Society

THE PERSISTENCE OF ETHNICITY IN THE SOVIET ERA[1]

Lenin believed that nations first emerged during the transition from feudalism to capitalism and that under Communism they would eventually fuse. Following the Revolution, however, the Bolsheviks took over an enormous country with over a hundred recognized national or ethnic groups[2] at various levels of economic development. They concluded that Soviet reality demanded the creation of a federal state with fifteen national republics and many smaller divisions (autonomous republics, autonomous regions and national districts), each associated with a particular ethnic group.

It was not until the Brezhnev era that some Soviet social scientists proclaimed the realization of Lenin's dream. A new community, "the Soviet people", had allegedly been forged out of the ethnic mixture inherited from the Tsars. Here is what some of the Soviet Union's leading students of ethnicity wrote at the time:

The natural social and economic integration of the peoples of the USSR is closely associated with their political integration within the framework of a single federal state which represents the organic harmony, and not simply a conglomerate of national-administrative units. The Programme of the CPSU points out that as social construction continues, the boundaries between the Union republics continue to lose their former significance. These fundamental changes signify that the national question, as inherited by the socialist state from the past epoch, has been resolved completely, finally and irrevocably.

Socio-economic and socio-political changes in the USSR have resulted in a new historical community, the Soviet people. . . . [3]

Wooden phrases notwithstanding, there was an element of truth in these claims. After 1917 a growing proportion of the Soviet population learned to speak Russian. Economic inequalities between the myriad national groups diminished. Regionally, economies were unified and placed

6

under central control, while homologous stratification systems crystallized. A country-wide educational system and curriculum were established. Monopolistic mass media broadcast uniform "truths". Remarkable national achievements, such as victory in World War II, galvanized the people and unified them against a "common enemy". Other accomplishments, such as the national space programme, served as a focus for their pride. Common lifestyles were adopted by many citizens, regardless of their ethnic origin. Some members of the national groups most recently incorporated into the USSR resented Sovietization. But to a degree—in some cases, to a large degree—people *did* come to think of themselves as part of "a new historical community, the Soviet people".

Contrary to the claims of the late Brezhnev era, however, the "national question" was not "resolved completely, finally and irrevocably". Far from it. The great paradox of ethnicity in the Soviet Union was that alongside the abovementioned integrative and assimilative pressures, precisely opposite forces throve. This was because ethnicity was used as one of the most important criteria by which people were recruited to higher educational institutions, professional and administrative positions and political posts.[4]

Soviet nationality policy was developed as a means of securing the loyalty of the professional classes in the republics to the political centre and thereby preventing ethnic separatism. Members of ethnic groups residing in their own national republics were given special privileges; elite and professional recruitment was based partly on territorial-ethnic principles. Those residing outside their designated homelands (e.g. Russians in Estonia, Uzbeks in Kyrgyzstan) and especially those without designated homelands (e.g. Jews, ethnic Germans)[5] came to be permanently disadvantaged as a matter of state policy.

The system of territorical-ethnic recruitment first took shape as early as the 1930s. A corollary of Stalin's heretical decision to create "socialism in one country" was the need for iron discipline. This entailed purging all regional elites and replacing them with indigenous Party loyalists. Around the same time, Stalin instituted the internal passport system. Although originally conceived as a mechanism for preventing peasants from escaping collective farms, internal passports soon became the administrative means by which ethnic recruitment was carried out. Each person over the age of fifteen was obliged to carry an internal passport listing, among other things, his or her nationality. Over the years, and especially as attempts were made to invigorate growth in underdeveloped regions, ethnicity became critically important in determining where and what one would study and where and at what one would work. Soviet federalism made ethnicity one of the most salient bases of social mobility and immobility.

The following tables help substantiate the argument presented above. In 1979 Rasma Karklins, an American political scientist, conducted a survey in West Germany of 176 ethnic German immigrants from the Soviet Union.[6] Among other questions, she asked her respondents what criteria were in their opinions most important in facilitating access to higher education. The results varied by the respondent's region of origin. As Table 2.1 shows, however, nationality was perceived to be the overwhelmingly important criterion in Kazakhstan and the four republics of Central Asia and very important indeed in Russia and the three Baltic republics. Nationality was far and away the single most frequently mentioned criterion perceived to determine access to higher education in all republics.

Karklins also participated in the 1983 Soviet Interview Project, which involved a survey of Soviet immigrants in the United States, over 83 per cent of whom were Jews.[7] Among other questions, each respondent was asked who in his or her republic was treated best in terms of access to political positions, jobs, and higher education—Russians or members of the titular nationality (Ukrainians in Ukraine, etc.). Table 2.2 gives the results for the 924 respondents who answered the question. Only among respondents from Latvia and Belarus did fewer than 40 per cent think that members of the titular nationality were favoured in recruitment to political positions, jobs and higher education. In Ukraine, Georgia and Armenia the corresponding figure was in the neighbourhood of 50 per cent. In the remaining republics—Russia, Kazakhstan, the four republics of Soviet Central Asia, Lithuania, Estonia and Moldova—a huge majority was convinced that titular nationality mattered above all else in determining the allocation of political positions, jobs and places in the system of higher education.

Part of Table 2.3 illustrates in broad strokes the consequences of these policies. Column 1 gives the proportion of people in each republic who were members of the titular nationality in 1989, the year of the last Soviet census. Column 2 gives the proportion of people in each republic's administrative-managerial cadres who were members of the titular nationality in 1989. Subtracting the numbers in column 2 from the corresponding numbers in column 1, we see that in nine of the fifteen republics the titular nationality was overrepresented among administrative-managerial personnel (as indicated by the plus signs in column 2). In five other republics the degree of underrepresentation (indicated by the minus signs in column 2) was small—an average of 1.7 per cent. Only in tiny, agricultural Moldova were members of the titular nationality significantly

Table 2.1

Criteria Mentioned as Facilitating Access to Higher Education, Soviet German Immigrants in West Germany, by Region, 1979 (in per cent; n=176)

	Russia	Baltic	Central Asia	Kazakhstan	Other
nationality only	33	39	68	82	50
nationality and other factors	17	4	12	7	11
other factors only	50	57	20	11	39
total	100	100	100	100	100

Source: Rasma Karklins, *Ethnic Relations in the USSR: The Perspective from Below* (London: Unwin Hyman, 1986), 64.

Table 2.2

Perceptions of Nationalities Treated Best, Soviet Immigrants in USA, by Region, 1983 (in per cent; n=924)

	Political positions		Jobs		Higher education	
	Russians	titular	Russians	titular	Russians	titular
Azerbaydzhan	4	87	4	83	4	92
Russia	88	88	81	81	84	84
Lithuania, Estonia	7	83	8	56	7	76
Kazakhstan, Central Asia	4	76	1	71	3	71
Moldova	20	68	11	77	5	61
Georgia, Armenia	11	63	4	52	5	43
Ukraine	27	52	20	51	27	47
Latvia	40	35	32	20	45	28
Belarus	35	32	21	31	29	25

Source: Adapted from Rasma Karklins, "Nationality policy and ethnic relations in the USSR" in James R. Millar (ed.), *Politics, Work, and Daily Life in the USSR: A Survey of Former Soviet Citizens* (Cambridge UK: Cambridge University Press, 1987), 305-7.

Table 2.3
Ethnic Heterogeneity in the Soviet Republics, 1989

	proportion titular nationals of total republic population	proportion titular nationals of total administrative-managerial personnel in republic (over- or underrepresentation in parentheses)		proportion non-republic residents of all titular nationals (millions in parentheses)	
Russia	81.5	77.3	(- 4.2)	17.4	(25.3)
Ukraine	72.7	79.0	(+ 6.3)	15.3	(6.8)
Belarus	77.9	77.7	(- .2)	21.2	(2.1)
Moldova	64.5	49.8	(-14.7)	16.0	(.6)
Lithuania	79.6	91.5	(+11.9)	4.7	(.1)
Latvia	52.0	63.1	(+11.1)	4.9	(.1)
Estonia	61.5	82.2	(+20.7)	6.2	(.1)
Georgia	70.1	89.3	(+19.2)	4.9	(.2)
Armenia	93.3	99.4	(+ 6.1)	25.7	(1.1)
Azerbaydzhan	82.7	93.8	(+11.1)	14.3	(1.0)
Kazakhstan	39.7	39.5	(- .2)	19.7	(1.6)
Uzbekistan	71.4	67.6	(- 3.8)	15.3	(2.6)
Turkmenistan	72.0	71.8	(- .2)	7.0	(.2)
Tadzhikistan	62.3	66.3	(+ 4.0)	24.7	(1.0)
Kyrgyzstan	52.4	55.1	(+ 2.7)	11.8	(.3)

Sources: Adapted from John P. Cole and Igor V. Filatotchev, "Some observations on migration within and from the former USSR in the 1990s", *Post-Soviet Geography*, vol. 33, no. 7, 1992, 440, 444; L. L. Ribakovsky and N. V. Tarasova, "Migration processes in the USSR: New phenomena", *Sotsiologicheskiye issledovaniya*, no. 7, 1990, 40.

underrepresented (by 14.7 per cent). On average, titular nationalities were overrepresented by nearly 5 per cent in their republics' administrative-managerial personnel. This is remarkable, especially given the underdeveloped state of Soviet Central Asia and Kazakhstan seventy years earlier. Clearly, the territorial-ethnic basis of recruitment had worked well. It had served as a mechanism for allocating privilege and indulgence.[8] Of course, it therefore necessarily served also as a mechanism for allocating underprivilege and resentment. As a result, and despite more than seven decades of Sovietization, ethnic identity was prominent and smouldering on the eve of the collapse of the Communist system in 1991. This was especially evident in the case of the Jews.

THE JEWISH DILEMMA[9]

Under the Communist regime, the Jews were at first a privileged minority to some degree. In a country still consisting largely of illiterate peasants, they were relatively urbanized and educated. In a country whose new rulers were intent on excluding, expelling and killing many members of the old educated classes on grounds of disloyalty, they were disproportionately faithful to the new regime, which many of them saw as their salvation from discrimination and pogroms. In a country whose dominant idea was equality they were viewed by some officials as members of a persecuted minority who deserved special advantages. For all these reasons the Jews advanced quickly in the new Soviet hierarchy.

By 1926 the social structure of the Jewish community had altered considerably. In 1897 a plurality of the Jewish labour force, fully 31 per cent, consisted of merchants, nearly all of them economically marginal. Twenty-nine years later merchants constituted only 12 per cent of the labour force. The proportion of agricultural workers had quadrupled. The proportion of salaried nonmanual workers had more than doubled. Between 1926 and 1935 the number of manual workers tripled.

Jews were particularly attracted to occupations demanding high levels of education. By 1970 they were by far the most highly educated group in the USSR. Some 239 out of every 1,000 Jews over the age of ten had a university education in that year. That compares with a mere 62 out of 1,000 for the entire population and 155 out of 1,000 for Georgians, the second-ranked group. In 1973, when the Jews represented only about 1 per cent of the population, they comprised nearly 2 per cent of university students in the USSR, over 6 per cent of all scientific workers, nearly 9 per cent of all scientists, and 14 per cent of all Doctors of Science (the equivalent of a full professorship in North America). In absolute terms, the only ethnic group with more Doctors of Science than the 2 million Jews were the 130 million Russians. In Moscow, the intellectual capital, Jews comprised nearly 14 per cent of all scientists and over 17 per cent of all Doctors of Science. This extraordinary profile is reflected in Table 2.4, which shows the educational and occupational attainment of the respondents in my sample. Fewer than a tenth of the respondents are manual workers.

Over two-thirds have at least some university education. Six per cent have earned a PhD or higher.

These figures demonstrate that within two generations of the Revolution the Jews of the Soviet Union had been transformed from a destitute and persecuted minority, comprising mainly economically marginal merchants and artisans in Ukraine and Belarus, into the country's most highly educated and urbanized ethnic group, a plurality of whose members had

Table 2.4
Respondents by Education and Occupation

education	frequency	per cent
less than 7 years	3	0
7-8 years	10	1
9-11 years	131	13
professional-technical school	39	4
technical school	140	14
at least some university	615	62
PhD	51	5
Doctor of Science	9	1
total	998	100

occupation	frequency	per cent
manual worker	56	9
teacher	51	8
government service	44	7
private manager	96	15
entrepreneur	30	5
scientist	49	7
engineer	207	32
physician	35	5
lawyer	8	1
free professional	40	6
government administrator	38	6
other	3	0
total	657	101

Note: Percentages do not necessarily total 100 due to rounding.

moved to the Russian heartland. The fact that, practically speaking, they possessed no territory of their own[10] initially operated to their advantage: they were a facile group whose members could easily be mobilized by the regime to play special modernizing functions in a country initially lacking intellectual resources.

The price for this unprecedented upward social mobility was the virtual destruction of Jewish culture. In 1913 Lenin wrote that anyone who supported the idea of Jewish national culture was an enemy of the proletariat. That attitude did not preclude state support for elements of culture that were (according to the Bolshevik formula) national in form but socialist in content. Consequently, throughout the 1920s those modes of Jewish political and cultural expression which supported the regime were tolerated and even fortified—Yiddish-language newspapers, public schools, proletarian theatre, literature and art, Jewish Sections of the Communist Party, Jewish soviets, and so forth. All these institutions were directed at enforcing pro-Communist tendencies in the Jewish community—and at eliminating Judaism and Zionism from the Jewish cultural repertoire. Thus despite state support for Jewish proletarian culture, thousands of Jewish schools and synagogues were closed in the 1920s.

By 1930 Stalin had initiated a policy of homogenizing all politics and culture and harnessing them to the single aim of building socialism in one country. His campaigns against various deviations from the Party line and the ensuing purges touched many national groups. They affected Jews disproportionately because they were so heavily involved in Party affairs. In addition, most official Jewish institutions were shut down by 1938. The brief flowering of Jewish proletarian culture was over.

The strength of Jewish cultural life in the Soviet Union was briefly invigorated in 1939-40. Under the terms of the Molotov-Ribbentrop pact the Soviet Union annexed the Baltic states and parts of Poland and Romania together with their large Jewish populations. There were now more than 5 million Jews in the USSR and 60 per cent of them had no experience of the homogenizing effects of more than two decades of Soviet rule. However, only half the Jews in the Soviet Union survived the Nazi genocide machine. And due mainly to rural antisemitism, the Jews from the western territories who remained alive after World War II tended to migrate to the larger cities of the region and to Russia proper. There assimilative processes operated in full force.

From 1946 to 1953 Stalin launched a series of campaigns against the Jews who, although never named directly, were singled out by means of codewords—"rootless cosmopolitans", "bourgeois nationalists", "plotters against Stalin" and the like. The remaining fragments of organized Jewish life were now swept away and the community's leading cultural figures shot or sent to die a slower death in remote prison camps.

A crusade against "economic criminals", initiated by Khrushchev in 1961 and lasting three years, had unmistakable antisemitic overtones. And a sustained battle against "international Zionists" was waged by Brezhnev's regime in the wake of the Arab-Israeli war in 1967.

State-sponsored antisemitism became more intense when it was expedient for the regime and less intense when it served no useful purpose. But underlying the emergence of state-sponsored antisemitism in the first place was the simple reality that the Jews did not fit into the grand scheme of Soviet nationality policy, with its emphasis on the proportional representation of titular nationalities in administrative, professional and scientific positions. The central leadership judged that social stability could be bolstered if Jewish professionals were replaced by members of the titular nationalities, thus securing the fealty of the latter and preventing their involvement in republic nationalisms.

As early as the 1930s some replacements became available. Stalin initiated the widespread educational upgrading of *vydvizhentsy*, or workers "from the bench", and their recruitment to precisely the sorts of jobs in which Jews figured prominently. Khrushchev proudly noted that the Soviets had "created new cadres" and explained that "[i]f the Jews now want to occupy the top jobs in our republics, they would obviously be looked upon unfavourably by the indigenous peoples."[11]

But it was really only in the period 1967-71 that large numbers of Jews began to wonder whether they and their children had any future in the USSR. Many memoirs and systematic studies from that period show that Jews began to face sharply restricted educational and professional opportunities at that time. Here is just one contemporary example of the operation of ethnic quotas. In 1979 there were 47 non-Jewish and 40 Jewish student applicants to the Mechanics and Mathematics Department of Moscow State University. The non-Jews had won 26 mathematics Olympiads, the Jews 48, yet 40 non-Jews and only six Jews were accepted into the Department.[12] These and similar circumstances were repeated countless times, especially in the better schools and institutes. This is one of the most important reasons why some Jews began to consider the difficult process of emigrating. Their lives in the Soviet Union were based on their ability to achieve professional excellence. When opportunities to excel professionally were restricted, they felt that there was no future for them in the USSR.

The anomalous position of the Jews in the structure of Soviet nationality relations was the most fundamental reason for the emergence of the emigration movement. But it was not the only reason. The United States of America and other Western governments began to use whatever influence they could muster, including trade sanctions, to encourage the Soviet authorities to permit some Jews to leave. Isreal's victory in the 1967 Six Day War stimulated a feeling of pride, defiance and Zionist activism among some Soviet Jews. The "anti-Zionist" ideological and political campaign, with its antisemitic excesses, launched by the regime to counter the philosophy and practice of emigration convinced many Jews that they no longer had a place in Soviet society and that they should abandon all hope of political and cultural reform. Thus the emigration movement grew in response to a unique conjuncture of structural circumstances, precipitants and motivations.

The emigration movement began haltingly in 1966 and in earnest in 1971. Until 1977 most of the emigrants were inspired to leave by Zionist and religious motives. Most of them came from peripheral areas where assimilation was less widespread, notably the Baltics, Moldova, western Ukraine, western Belarus (all of which fell under Soviet rule only after World War II) and Georgia. Most of the emigrants went to Israel. By 1977, however, a change in the nature of the movement was signalled by the fact that, for the first time, more than half the emigrants chose to go to the United States and other Western countries rather than Israel. Thereafter, most Jews left for less ideological and more pragmatic reasons—to enjoy political and cultural freedom, to escape the burden of being a Jew in the Soviet Union, to join family members, to ensure a secure future for their children and, especially from the end of the 1980s, to flee political instability and economic ruin. A growing proportion of emigrants now came from the Russian heartland and eastern Ukraine and Belarus: they were relatively assimiliated Jews whose families had lived under Communism since 1917, who had passed through the Soviet education system and who thought of Russian culture as their own.

Indeed, many relatively assimilated Jews—Ted Friedgut refers to them as the "silent majority"[13]—decided not to emigrate at all. They tried their best to accomodate themselves to the realities of the Brezhnev years and the new uncertainties of life under Gorbachev and Yeltsin. Many were simply confused about who they were and what they should do. One contemporary lamented:

Who am I now? Who do I feel myself to be? Unfortunately, I do not feel like a Jew. I understand that I have an unquestionable genetic tie with

Jewry. I also assume that this is reflected in my mentality, in my mode of thinking, and in my behavior. But this common quality is as little help to me in feeling my Jewish identity as similarity of external features— evidently, a more profound, or more general, common bond is lacking, such as community of language, culture, history, tradition. . . .

I am accustomed to the color, smell, rustle, of the Russian land- scape, as I am to the Russian language, the rhythm of Russian poetry. I react to everything else as an alien. . . .

And nevertheless, no, I am not Russian, I am a stranger today in this land.[14]

The marginality that characterizes the Jews of the region, their uncer- tainty as to where they belong, their cultural and geographical suspension, as it were between East and West, has made them ideal political pawns. In the Cold War era they were used (if I may mix metaphors) as bargaining chips in US-Soviet relations. In the swift economic and political decline that has characterized the CIS over the past few years, antisemites have cast them as devious and powerful conspirators against the once-mighty empire. Israeli officials have been inclined to give high estimates of their numbers and distort their motives for emigrating. Many Jews in Israel and the West perceive tremendous potential in the region for a revival of Jewish culture and have generously donated personnel and resources to facilitate that re- birth. Clearly, these and other groups have strong vested interests in char- acterizing the Jews of the region in one way or another. The desire to sort out competing depictions is sufficient justification for wanting to listen systematically to what the remaining Jews of the region have to say about themselves. In my judgement, the survey results reported in the following pages represent one of the most finely tuned listening devices available to date.

Let us now turn our attention to three of the questions which the survey can help answer. How many Jews now live in Russia, Ukraine and Belarus? How Jewish are they? Which factors determine variations in the degree of Jewishness typically found in different categories of the population?

NOTES

1   This section is a slightly revised version of Robert J. Brym, "From 'the Soviet people' to the refugee crisis in Russia" in Rozalina Ryvkina and Rostislav Turovskiy, *The Refugee Crisis in Russia*, Robert Brym (ed.), P. Patchet-Golubev, trans., (Toronto: York Lanes Press, 1993), 1-4.

2   I use the terms ethnicity and nationality interchangeably here.

3   J. Bromley *et al.*, *Present-Day Ethnic Processes in the USSR* (Moscow: Progress Publishers 1982 [1977]), 269-70.

4   Victor Zaslavsky and Robert J. Brym, *Soviet-Jewish Emigration and Soviet Nationality Policy* (London: Macmillan, 1983).

5   Birobidzhan, the officially designated Jewish autonomous region near China, is largely a fiction. Only 0.6 per cent of Soviet Jews lived there in 1989. See Felix Ryansky, "Jews and Cossacks in the Jewish Autonomous Region", *Refuge*, vol. 12, no. 4, 1992, 19-21.

6   Rasma Karklins, *Ethnic Relations in the USSR: The Perspective from Below* (London: Unwin Hyman, 1986).

7   Rasma Karklins, "Nationality policy and ethnic relations in the USSR" in James R. Millar (ed.), *Politics, Work, and Daily Life in the USSR: A Survey of Former Soviet Citizens* (Cambridge UK: Cambridge University Press, 1987), 305-31.

8   This is not to suggest that ultimate power ever resided in the hands of the titular nationalities. Slavs, and Russians in particular, dominated the central apparatus and were nominally second-in-command in all republics.

9   The following sketch is based mainly on Mordechai Altshuler, "The Jewish Community in the Soviet Union: A Socio-Demographic Analysis" (Jerusalem: Magnes Press, Hebrew University of Jerusalem, 1979) (in Hebrew); Jonathan Frankel, "The Soviet regime and anti-Zionism: An analysis" in Yaacov Ro'i and Avi Beker (eds.), *Jewish Culture and Identity in the Soviet Union* (New York and London: New York University Press, 1991), 310-54; Yehoshua A. Gilboa, *The Black Years of Soviet Jewry, 1939-1953*, translated by Yosef Shachter and Dov Ben-Abba, (Boston: Little, Brown, 1971); Zvi Gitelman, *Jewish Nationality and Soviet Politics: The Jewish Sections of the CPSU, 1917-1930* (Princeton: Princeton University Press, 1972); Solomon M. Schwarz, *The Jews in the Soviet Union* (Syracuse NY: Syracuse University Press, 1951); and Zaslavsky and Brym.

10   See note 5.

11   "Meetings between representatives of the French Socialist Party and Soviet leaders (1956)" in Benjamin Pinkus (ed.), *The Soviet Government and the Jews 1948-1967* (Cambridge UK: Cambridge University Press, 1984), 58.

12   Moscow Helsinki Monitoring Group, *Discrimination Against Jews Enrolling at Moscow State University, 1979*, Document 112 (n.p.: 5 November 1979, mimeograph).

13   Theodore Friedgut, "Soviet Jewry: The silent majority", *Soviet Jewish Affairs*, vol. 10, no. 2, 1980, 3-19.

14   Larisa Bogoraz, "Do I feel I belong to the Jewish people?" in Aleksandr
      Voronel, Viktor Yakhot and Moshe Decter (eds.), *I am a Jew: Essays on
      Jewish Identity in the Soviet Union* (New York: Academic Committee on
      Soviet Jewry and Anti-Defamation League of B'nai B'rith, 1973), 63-4.

3 Identity

HOW MANY JEWS LIVE IN RUSSIA, UKRAINE AND BELARUS?

Estimates of the number of Jews in the former Soviet Union range from about 3 million to well under 1 million.[1] The low estimates are based on a strict interpretation of census returns. The high estimates are based on the assumption that an enormous number of Soviet citizens concealed their Jewish roots under the Soviet regime. Presumably, those people are now free to identify as Jews and, increasingly, do just that. In my judgement, neither estimate is accurate although census figures are much closer to the mark.

Three more or less well-known facts need to be reviewed before I offer my own population estimate.

- Like all citizens of the former Soviet Union over the age of fifteen, Jews are still required to hold an internal passport listing, among other things, the bearer's nationality, or what in the West is known as ethnicity. All children whose parents are Jewish according to their internal passports are themselves automatically registered as Jews. They cannot normally change their nationality designation, even as adults. In the survey on which this study is based, only 3 per cent of respondents said they had ever changed the nationality designation in their internal passports. Sixteen of the thirty cases involved a change to Russian nationality, ten to Jewish nationality and two each to Ukrainian and Belarusian.

- At the age of sixteen the child of a mixed marriage must choose one parent's nationality as his or her own. Research conducted during the Soviet period shows that adolescents chose the non-Jewish nationality in more than 90 per cent of cases. The number of children who made that choice is large, partly because the rate of ethnic intermarriage has been high and is getting higher. According to 1979 census figures, 47 per cent of Russian Jews lived in ethnically heterogeneous families. The corresponding figure for Ukrainian Jews was 33 per cent and for Belarusian Jews 29 per cent.[2]

19

According to 1988 marriage registration statistics, the percentage of mixed marriages in all marriages involving at least one Jewish spouse was 63 per cent in Russia, 45 per cent in Ukraine and 40 per cent in Belarus.[3] In my 1993 survey, the weighted proportion of ever-married respondents reporting a non-Jewish spouse is 60 per cent—61 per cent in Moscow, 58 per cent in Kiev, and 52 per cent in Minsk.

▪ Censuses were taken on an irregular basis in the Soviet Union. In principle, they presented Jews with an opportunity to deny their national origins. However, in the 1970s researchers in Israel sought to determine whether Soviet Jewish immigrants concealed their Jewish identity from Soviet census-takers. They discovered that people registered as Jews in their internal passports tended virtually unanimously to declare Jewish as their nationality in the census.[4] It is therefore commonly assumed that census figures are a good indicator of the number of passport Jews.

In the light of these facts, what can one make of the high and low estimates of Jewish population size? The high population estimates are generally based on the Israeli Law of Return, which offers immediate citizenship to all first or second generation offspring of Jews—defined as the offspring of Jewish mothers or converts—and to members of their households. Some demographers suggest that although the 1989 census counted 1.45 million Jews in the USSR, the actual number is more like 2.9 million if one takes into account "peripheral Jews"—non-Jewish spouses and the children and grandchildren of Jewish mothers who did not have their offpsring registered as Jews in their internal passports.

This estimate may be credible, but it is not very useful. An anthropologist once wrote that if any two people are chosen at random from the planet then on average they will be thirty-second cousins. This may underscore the common origins of all humanity but it does not greatly help us to understand geopolitical conflict among nations today. Analogously, inflated estimates of the number of Jews in the CIS may be of academic or political interest but if one is interested in ascertaining how many Jews are likely to become part of a functioning Jewish community or to emigrate it is necessary to be more realistic.

The plain fact is that many spouses of Jews have no interest in Jewish culture and no interest in leaving their country. Most children and especially grandchildren of Jewish mothers who did not have their offpsring registered as Jews are completely assimilated into Russian culture and also prefer to stay. That is evident from a recent study conducted by the Israeli

Ministry of the Interior. The Ministry issues identification cards to new citizens. It defines a Jew as anyone who was born to a Jewish mother, converted to Judaism, or can present a valid document issued by a legitimate civil authority testifying to the bearer's Jewish nationality. Between October 1989 and February 1991 only 6.4 per cent of 180,754 Soviet immigrants to Israel were not Jews, so defined.[5] While the proportion of non-Jews among all emigrants is somewhat higher (see below), these figures show that only a small minority of the 1.45 million or so peripheral Jews have so far emigrated and suggest that few will do so in the future. Since the main advantage of re-identifying oneself as a Jew is emigrating, far fewer are likely to become involved with the Jewish community in the CIS.

Population estimates at the low end adhere closely to census figures. They thereby ignore the undeniable tendency of some first-generation children of mixed marriages who are registered as non-Jews to re-identify as Jews. This, too, strikes me as untenable. Even under circumstances more stable than those which have characterized the region over the past few years, ethnicity is a somewhat plastic feature of one's identity, especially for people who do not associate very strongly with any one ethnic group.[6] Ethnic identity may change when circumstances and opportunities warrant it and, like members of all other ethnic groups, Jews in the former USSR have to a degree been influenced by pragmatic considerations in choosing their ethnicity. Thus when it was clearly disadvantageous to be registered as a Jew in one's internal passport on account of restricted education and employment opportunities, the children of mixed marriages tended overwhelmingly to register as non-Jews. In contrast, one big advantage has been bound up with Jewish ethnicity since the beginning of the emigration movement: many Jews have been able to obtain a one-way ticket out of the country. Hence the well-known Russian quip that defines a Jewish wife as a means of transportation. Some children of mixed marriages who were registered as non-Jews at the age of sixteen are now declaring that they are Jews.[7] Some of them emigrate. I estimate that in the last few years 15 per cent of all emigrants who declared themselves Jewish were in fact not Jewish according to their internal passports.[8]

If the possibility of emigration has inflated the number of self-proclaimed Jews in what is now the CIS, then by how much? Surveys can help answer that question. In selecting a sample of Jews to be interviewed for this study I decided to cast a wide net with fine mesh. I included in my sample only those people who said they were registered as Jews in their internal passports; *or* who said that their mothers or fathers were so registered; *or* who said they had a Jewish identity or a mixture of Jewish and

some other ethnic identity. The sample thus contains Jews defined by di-
verse criteria. Some of the respondents are marginally Jewish. Some of
them are not registered as Jews in their internal passports.

This is what makes it possible to estimate how many Jews lived in
Russia, Ukraine and Belarus in 1993. Assume that the 1,000 people in my
sample represent the broadest credible definition of the Jewish population
in those three countries. Since 6 per cent of the respondents said they were
registered as Jews in their internal passports and 31 per cent said that they
were not (see Table 3.1), we can calculate that the internal passport criterion underestimates the maximum size of the Jewish population by 46 per
cent (31/69). Of course, this refers only to the Jewish population of Moscow, Kiev and Minsk. Most of the rest of the former USSR—smaller centres in the Slavic republics, Moldova, the Baltic republics, and Central
Asia—has been less affected by assimilation. If these other centres were
included in the sample the underestimate would undoubtedly be smaller,
perhaps 35 per cent.

If we knew how many people in the entire population were registered
as Jews in their internal passports, we could add 35 per cent to that number
to arrive at a rough estimate of the size of the Jewish population, very
broadly defined. Fortunately, as we have seen, there exists an accurate estimate of how many people were registered as Jews in their internal passports in 1989. It is found in the census of that year. The way to estimate the
size of the Jewish population in Russia, Ukraine and Belarus in 1993 is thus
clear: (1) Find the Jewish population size according to the 1989 census; (2)
Subtract 85 per cent of the number of emigrants from 1989 to 1992 inclusive (all those registered as Jews); (3) Subtract the population loss during
that period due to causes other than emigration, notably the excess of
deaths over births; (4) Inflate that figure by 35 per cent.

According to the 1989 census, the Jewish population of the entire
USSR was 1,449,000.[9] Some 623,000 people who declared themselves as
Jews emigrated from 1989 to 1992 inclusive. Assuming that 85 per cent of
the emigrants were registered as Jews in their internal passports, this outflow brought the Jewish census population down to 919,000. In the 1980s
the rate of population decline due to factors other than emigration was 2.0
per cent.[10] Assuming that the rate did not change in the early 1990s, this
brought the census population down to 848,000 by 1993. Adding 35 per
cent to that figure, we arrive at a rough 1993 estimate of 1,144,000 people
in the entire territory of the former USSR who identified themselves as
Jews, were registered as Jews in their internal passports, or who had at least
one parent who was so registered.

In 1989 38 per cent of all Soviet Jews lived in Russia, 34 per cent in Ukraine and 8 per cent in Belarus. Assuming that those proportions remained constant until 1993, the Jewish population of Russia in 1993 was 435,000. For Ukraine the figure was 389,000 and for Belarus 92,000. Thus a realistic estimate of the maximum size of the total Jewish population in the three countries in 1993 is approximately 916,000. Applying the same logic to the three cities surveyed, in 1993 there were roughly 139,000 Jews in Moscow, 85,000 in Kiev and 31,000 in Minsk (see Table 3.2).

Table 3.1
Respondents by Nationality According to
Internal Passports (in per cent)

Jewish	69
Russian	22
Ukrainian	7
Belarusian	1
other	1
total	100

Table 3.2
Estimated Number of People Registered as Jewish, with At Least One Parent
Registered as Jewish, or Jewish Self-Identity, 1993

Russia	435,000	of which Moscow	139,000
Ukraine	389,000	of which Kiev	85,000
Belarus	92,000	of which Minsk	31,000
subtotal	916,000		
rest of former USSR	228,000		
total	1,144,000		

HOW JEWISH ARE THEY?

Now that we have a better idea of the size of the population about which I wish to generalize, I must emphasize that Jewish or any other ethnicity involves more than just identity. It also comprises a bundle of related beliefs and practices.[11] Accordingly, each respondent was asked nearly two dozen questions about his or her Jewish identity, beliefs and practices. The responses to those questions are presented in Table 3.3. Where data on roughly comparable items are available, the results of American and Canadian surveys conducted in 1989 and 1990 are set alongside the CIS results.[12] They help keep the CIS results in perspective.

What do all these numbers mean? Do they add up to a revival of Jewish communal life or a community in decline? The absence of comparable data from an earlier period makes it impossible to answer that question conclusively. However, several relevant observations are possible. First, any reasonably knowledgeable observer would have to be surprised that the values of three indicators of Jewish involvement are so high. The proportion of Jews who at least occasionally read the Jewish press (42 per cent) is higher than the comparable proportion in the USA (33 per cent). The proportion who celebrate Passover (42 per cent), while substantially less than the figures for North America (76 per cent for the USA and 92 per cent for Canada), is still remarkably high given the suppression of Judaism in the Soviet Union for so many years. (The popularity of Passover may be related to the frequently drawn parallel between the Biblical exodus from Egypt and the modern emigration movement.) And the fact that fully 73 per cent of Jews in Moscow, Kiev and Minsk express the desire to have more contact with Jewish culture must surely suggest that some potential for communal revival exists in those cities.

On the other hand, the data show a disturbing discrepancy between belief and practice, or between what Zvi Gitelman analagously calls "passive" and "active" Jewish identity. In his words:

> For most Jews, passive Jewish identity is associated with passive involvement with Jewish culture. For a minority, passive identity turns into active identity, which, in turn, leads to attempts to live actively as cultural Jews, whether defined religiously, linguistically, artistically, or in other ways. . . . Active culture is developed by minorities, but the size of those minorities and the ratio between active and passive identity vary with the fluctuations in Soviet conditions: in times of great pressure, such as 1948-53, the proportion of active identifiers, and

Table 3.3
Indicators of Jewishness Moscow/Kiev/Minsk, USA and Canada (in per cent)

question		Moscow/ Kiev/Minsk	USA	Canada
	general ideological statements			
q70.	Wants Jewish cultural revival	95		
q62.	Wants Jewish religious development	78		
q47.	National identification Jewish or Jewish and other	75		
	average	83		
	specific ideological statements			
q69.	Too little contact with Jewish culture	73		
q68.	Too little contact with other Jews	35		
q72.	Prefers that Jews marry other Jews	26		
q108.	Feels that Israel is the historical motherland of the Jewish people	24		
q56.	Plans to learn Hebrew or Yiddish	20		
q158.	Thinks of living in Israel as very important or important	19	13	21
	average	33		
	behavioural statements			
q65.	Often or occasionally reads Jewish press	42	33	60
q60.	Celebrates Passover	42	76	92
q44.	Spouse's nationality Jewish	40		90
q61.	Attends synagogue often or occasionally	33	50	67
q67.	Do you belong to Jewish community?	27		
q58.	Celebrates Jewish New Year	17		
q59.	Celebrates Day of Atonement	16	64	77
q73.	Bringing up children with Jewish traditions	16		
q57.	Celebrates Jewish Sabbath	10	26	54
q50.	Speaks Yiddish well or moderately well	8		37
q63.	Participates in Jewish organization	6	24	31
q64.	Member of Jewish organization	5	37	47
q49.	Speaks Hebrew well or moderately well	2		25
	average	20		

the amount of overt cultural activity, decline. In times of relative relaxation, such as the mid-1970s, active identity and culture grow, especially if external forces feed them.[13]

Surely the Jews of the region are now experiencing the greatest relaxation of state pressure against them since 1917. What then is the ratio of active to passive Jews or, as I would prefer to put it, how large is the discrepancy between belief and practice? In order to answer this question I divided the questionnaire items in Table 3.3 into three categories—general ideological statements (what the Americans call "motherhood issues"), specific ideological assertions, and declarations about actual Jewish practice. One immediately notices the very large proportion of respondents who agree with "motherhood issues". Nearly everyone wants a Jewish cultural revival to take place in their country and over three-quarters of the respondents would like to witness the invigorated development of Judaism.

Before concluding that this demonstrates a vast untapped potential for Jewish cultural rebirth in the Slavic republics of the CIS, however, one should bear in mind an important fact. Ever since polling has been conducted in the region, researchers have discovered that enormous proportions of the population agree with general principles that are in vogue. For example, nearly everyone—from die-hard Stalinists to Thatcherite conservatives—endorsed *perestroyka* in 1988. What they meant by *perestroyka* is, however, a different matter. Pollsters had to ask more specific questions about political and economic beliefs and practices before meaningful divisions of opinion emerged from their data.[14]

The same principle applies here. When respondents were asked about specific beliefs, the proportion choosing the more Jewish response dropped precipitously and large divisions of opinion materialized. For example, while 95 per cent of the respondents expressed the desire for a Jewish cultural revival, only 26 per cent said that it was important for Jews to marry other Jews. In general, the proportions dropped still further when respondents were asked about Jewish practice, such as whether they were bringing up their children in line with Jewish traditions (16 per cent) and whether they belonged to a Jewish organization (5 per cent). The average proportion of respondents giving a Jewish response on the three general ideological statements was 83 per cent. For the six specific ideological assertions, the average was only 33 per cent. For the thirteen declarations of Jewish practice, the average dropped to 20 per cent.

Fewer than a fifth of Jews in Moscow, Kiev and Minsk have a working knowledge of Hebrew or Yiddish, belong to or participate in a Jewish organization, have a Jewish upbringing, are giving a Jewish upbringing to their children, or celebrate the Sabbath or the High Holy Days. Moreover, with the single exception of reading the Jewish press, the participation rates of the respondents in all Jewish activities are well below the corresponding rates for the 5,500,000 Jews in the USA and far below the corresponding rates for the 370,000 Jews in Canada. In absolute and comparative terms, and speaking here only of group averages, these results indicate that the cultural and organizational infrastructures of the Jewish communities of Moscow, Kiev and Minsk embrace only a small fraction of the Jewish population. Specifically, only 27 per cent of the respondents feel that they are part of the Jewish community. I conclude that while there is a suprisingly widespread desire for a reanimation of Jewish life in Moscow, Kiev and Minsk, it is doubtful whether more than a third of the population wants to become personally involved.

Group averages always mask internal variations, and it is important to know which categories of the population are most inclined to give Jewish responses to the questionnaire items. It augurs well for Jewish communal life in the CIS if the respondents who are most actively involved in the community are likely to remain in the population in the near future. If, on the other hand, the most Jewish respondents turn out to be those who will soon leave the community—in particular, the elderly and emigrants—then its future is bleaker.

WHAT DETERMINES JEWISHNESS?

In order to answer this question I first constructed an index of Jewishness by combining twenty of the items listed in Table 3.3 and then dividing the index into high, medium and low values.[15] I selected cutoff points so that about a third of the sample falls into each of the three values. Table 3.4 shows how Jewishness varies by city, age and a host of other variables. Only relationships that are likely to occur by chance less than once in twenty times are shown; eleven of the fourteen relationships are likely to occur by chance less than once in 1,000 times.

Table 3.4 offers some obvious findings and some surprises. Consider first that level of education is not listed as a statistically significant predictor of Jewishness. A number of researchers, including L. M. Drobizheva and Zvi Gitelman, have emphasized that "the more educated strata are more likely to have more links to their ethnic groups than others. It is precisely more educated people who are more aware of membership in a

Table 3.4
Jewishness by Correlates (in per cent; n in parentheses)

		Jewishness		
question	low	medium	high	total
q5. city				
Moscow	38	33	29	100 (544)
Kiev	33	34	33	100 (333)
Minsk	12	31	57	100 (123)
chi-square = 47.79, d.f. = 4, sig. = .000, tau-c = .142				
q8. age				
18-29	41	25	33	100 (182)
30-39	30	37	33	100 (153)
40-49	37	33	30	100 (215)
50-59	31	37	32	100 (284)
60+	28	32	41	100 (167)
chi-square = 15.91, d.f. = 8, sig. = .043, tau-c = .065				
q48. exposure to Jewish culture in upbringing				
great	4	12	85	100 (26)
moderate	7	24	71	100 (102)
weak	19	37	44	100 (273)
negligible	46	34	20	100 (582)
chi-square = 179.36, d.f.=6, sig. = .000, tau-c = -.341				
q74. emigration plans				
yes	16	28	56	100 (288)
no	43	35	22	100 (572)
chi-square = 107.81, d.f.=2, sig. = .000, tau-c = -.357				
q42. father's passport nationality				
Jewish	28	35	37	100 (800)
other	56	26	19	100 (200)
chi-square = 57.56, d.f.=2, sig. = .000, tau-c = -.196				
q43. mother's passport nationality				
Jewish	21	37	42	100 (698)
other	61	24	14	100 (303)
chi-square = 162.32, d.f.=2, sig. = .000, tau-c = -.382				

Table 3.4 (cont'd)
Jewishness by Correlates (in per cent; n in parentheses)

q44. spouse's passport nationality

Jewish	27	31	42	100 (408)
other	38	34	28	100 (592)

chi-square = 22.88, d.f. = 2, sig. = .000, tau-c = -.158

q45. respondent's passport nationality

Jewish	21	37	42	100 (684)
other	60	25	15	100 (317)

chi-square = 150.62, d.f. = 2, sig. = .000, tau-c = -.373

q123. personally suffered antisemitism

yes	20	38	41	100 (553)
no	48	29	23	100 (328)

chi-square = 77.01, d.f. = 2, sig. = .000, tau-c = -.288

q130. fear antisemitism

very much	20	34	45	100 (297)
not very much	32	36	33	100 (385)
not at all	50	26	23	100 (270)

chi-square = 64.65, d.f. = 4, sig. = .000, tau-c = -.219

q40. occupational satisfaction

satisfied	40	31	28	100 (478)
wants higher	26	37	37	100 (380)

chi-square = 20.07, d.f. = 2, sig. = .000, tau-c = .153

q41. opportunities for upward mobility

yes	42	30	28	100 (178)
no	31	34	35	100 (629)

chi-square = 7.43, d.f. = 2, sig. = .024, tau-c = .081

q162. political system in 1-2 years

freer	39	33	27	100 (142)
same	33	32	35	100 (342)
less free	26	33	42	100 (240)

chi-square = 11.05, d.f. = 4, sig. = .026, tau-c = .107

q163. confidence in own future

yes	47	26	27	100 (162)
no	29	36	35	100 (701)

chi-square = 19.32, d.f. = 2, sig. = .000, tau-c = .106

community of fate."[16] They apparently based their conclusion on casual observation and/or data drawn from non-random samples of Jews. One inference that may be drawn from my survey is that education does *not* influence Jewishness. Less educated Jews are as likely as more educated Jews to have high levels of Jewish identity, belief and practice; being "more aware of membership in a community of fate" is not a luxury (or a burden) unique to the highly educated.[17]

City of residence, in contrast, does have a statistically significant effect on level of Jewishness. It is well known that Jews in the western part of the former Soviet Union are less assimiliated than those in eastern Ukraine and Russia proper because the western territory was incorporated in the USSR only after World War II. "Heartlanders" have had three decades more exposure to Communism than those on the periphery, which is why they are less Jewish. But even Kiev and Minsk, which have (with the exception of the World War II period) been under Russian control since the early years of Soviet rule, contain populations that are more actively involved in Jewish life than are the Jews of Moscow. There are two reasons for this. First, many Moscow Jews are descendants of people who arrived in the city from the western part of the USSR in the years immediately following the Revolution. Many of them were already quite highly assimilated when they arrived. In contrast, Jews from Kiev and especially Minsk are more likely to have arrived later from small centres in the region and to have been less assimilated when they migrated. Indeed, the families of many Jews in Kiev and Minsk left their villages for the city only after World War II. Second, Moscow is a larger and more cosmopolitan centre than Kiev; and Kiev is a larger and more cosmopolitan centre than Minsk. Assimilative pressures probably vary accordingly.

Table 3.4 also shows that people who are sixty years of age and older, and who were therefore more exposed to Jewish culture in their youth, are today more involved in Jewish life than people under the age of sixty, who have had less exposure to Jewish culture. Older Jews are more likely to have had religious or ethnically involved parents. Many secular Jewish institutions functioned until the 1930s. The impact of Jewish schools, theatres, publishing houses and newspapers is still evident among the older generation of Jews in Moscow, Kiev and Minsk.

The last finding may surprise observers of the Jewish scene in the CIS who believe that a widespread revival of Jewish culture is gripping the younger generation. There *is* a revival. However, it is not sufficiently extensive to show up in the survey data. The proportion of respondents between the ages of eighteen and fifty-nine who demonstrate high levels of Jewishness is nearly constant at 30 to 33 per cent. This is not an encouraging finding. In the next decade or two natural demographic processes will eliminate many of the people who are most actively involved in Jewish life in the three cities—those sixty years of age and older.

With the exception of the collapse of the Communist regime, the single most important event for Jews in the region in the past quarter-century was the onset of the emigration movement. As noted above, the very existence of the movement encouraged many people who previously had no connection with the community to redefine themselves as Jews. The data presented in Table 3.4 are certainly consistent with that interpretation. There is a strong association between planning to emigrate, on the one hand, and, on the other, demonstrating strong Jewish patterns of belief and high rates of community participation.[18] Here again we confront a discouraging indicator of communal longevity: the most "Jewish Jews" are planning to leave. Aleksandr Burakovsky, Chairman of the Kiev Sholem Aleichem Society, may have exaggerated only a little when he stated in 1992 "Twenty more years, and the Jews will be gone."[19]

The data also support the view that the persistence of Jewish identity, belief and practice has been encouraged by the internal passport regime. As we saw in Chapter 2, ethnicity was an important factor which helped determine the allocation of students to institutions of higher education. Ethnic quotas were also used to earmark personnel for managerial, professional and scientific positions. The internal passport regime was the administrative mechanism by which the system of ethnic recruitment was implemented. Its unintended consequence was to maintain the salience of ethnicity in general and Jewish ethnicity in particular. Little wonder, then, that in 1993 we should discover higher levels of Jewishness among people who are designated as Jews in their internal passports and whose mothers, fathers and spouses are also so designated.

In the aftermath of World War II Jean-Paul Sartre remarked that "it is the anti-Semite who creates the Jew."[20] Notwithstanding the one-sidedness of his argument, it does contain an element of truth, as Table 3.4 shows. Respondents who have personally suffered from antisemitism and respondents who fear antisemitism are more likely to express high levels of Jewishness than those who lack such experiences and anxieties. This argument is given additional, indirect support by the data on the age distribution of Jewishness. In general, the proportion of people expressing low levels of Jewishness varies inversely with age: younger Jews are more likely to express low levels of Jewishness than older Jews. The only exception is the

30-39 age cohort. Respondents in that age cohort are somewhat less likely to display a low level of Jewishness than expected. That may be because people in that age cohort were in their formative years during the especially virulent and protracted "anti-Zionist" campaigns of the late 1960s to early 1980s.[21]

Finally, Table 3.4 demonstrates that high levels of Jewishness are significantly related to a series of factors indicating a pessimistic outlook on one's future prospects in Moscow, Kiev and Minsk. Research conducted in the USA shows that, in general, ethnicity is reinforced among people who feel that they cannot advance on their individual merits.[22] Especially if they believe that discrimination against their ethnic group is an important reason for their blocked mobility, people tend to view their individual interests as identical with their group interests. They are then inclined to seek collective, ethnic means of improving their situation. These generalizations hold for the Jews in Moscow, Kiev and Minsk. The most Jewish Jews in those cities tend to express dissatisfaction with their current occupations, believe that they have few opportunities for upward occupational mobility, judge that the political system will give them fewer freedoms in the next year or two and in general hold a pessimistic outlook on their future in their country. Respondents who are less Jewishly involved tend not to be so occupationally and politically discouraged. They are therefore more inclined to seek individual rather than ethnic-group means of improving the conditions of their existence.

Table 3.4 lists all the variables in the questionnaire that are statistically significantly related to level of Jewishness. The list is informative, but only to a degree. The main trouble with it is that it gives us no idea of the *magnitude* of the *independent* effect of each variable on Jewishness. By "magnitude" I refer to the fact that each variable discussed above may weigh more or less heavily in determining how Jewish the respondents feel and act. Knowing exactly what causal weight to attach to each variable would represent an advance in our knowledge. By "independence" I refer to the fact that the effects of some variables on Jewishness may be wholly or partly explained by other variables. For example, age is significantly associated with Jewishness. But older people also tend to have had a more Jewish upbringing—and the nature of one's upbringing is also significantly associated with Jewishness. When one takes into account the causal weight of upbringing, how much causal effect is left for age? These and related questions can be answered by multiple regression analysis.

Table 3.5 presents a multiple regression of Jewishness on all of the variables listed in Table 3.4.[23] The standardized slopes (betas) listed in column 3 indicate the magnitude of each variable's independent effects compared to the magnitude of the other variables' independent effects.

We see from Table 3.5 that the single most important determinant of Jewishness is the degree to which one was exposed to Jewish culture during one's upbringing. Planning to emigrate has 72 per cent of the effect of upbringing in determining level of Jewishness. Having a mother with a Jewish passport designation and having a spouse with a Jewish passport designation exert, respectively, 50 and 44 per cent of the effect of upbringing on level of Jewishness. The remaining four variables--whether one personally experienced antisemitism, whether one's father has or had a Jewish passport designation, whether one fears antisemitism and one's city of residence--each exert between 28 and 31 per cent of the effect of upbringing on Jewishness.[24] Age and factors associated with perceptions of blocked mobility do not appear in the table because their effects are totally accounted for by these other variables.

Table 3.5
Multiple Regression of Jewishness

question	slope (b)	standard error	standardized slope (beta)	t
q48-Jewish upbringing	4.18	.33	.36	12.58
q74-emigration plans	4.92	.57	.26	8.62
q43-mother's passport	3.56	.62	.18	5.73
q44-spouse's passport	2.90	.54	.16	5.36
q123-experience antisemitism	1.95	.57	.10	3.44
q42-father's passport	2.29	.76	.10	3.16
q130-fear antisemitism	1.27	.35	.11	3.63
q5-city size	1.32	.39	.10	3.35

intercept = -37.85; n = 731; adjusted R^2 = .42

SUMMARY

About three-quarters of the people in my sample do not feel that they are connected to the Jewish community and about two-thirds of them do not wish to have any more contact with Jews. Many respondents are prepared to state rather vaguely that they would like to have more contact with Jewish culture, but when it comes to specifics the numbers fall sharply. Stated in absolute terms, there are roughly 255,000 Jews in the three cities but only about 85,000 of them are now, or are likely soon to become, part of the Jewish community in any meaningful sense. To this one must add the observation that Jewishness is stronger among those with emigration plans and among older respondents. Thus many of the 85,000 actual and potential community members will leave or die in the near future. On the basis of the information in hand one cannot be very optimistic that in ten or twenty years the cultural revival undoubtedly taking place in the region will engulf any more than a small minority of the Jews in Moscow, Kiev and Minsk.

Several factors emerge from my analysis as the main sources of Jewish identity, belief and practice in Moscow, Kiev and Minsk. They include Jewish upbringing, the possibility of emigration, the passport regime, antisemitism and city of residence. Taken together, these factors explain a very respectable 42 per cent of the variation in Jewishness among the respondents.

In terms of its causal weight, antisemitism ranks only fourth on this list of five factors. Arguably, however, it is the most volatile force on the list. Some commentators feel that the long history of antisemitism in the region, combined with the current economic and political instability of the CIS, could cause antisemitism to spread and Jewish identity to be strengthened as a result. In order to shed light on this question I will next analyze Jewish perceptions of antisemitism and the strength and distribution of antisemitic sentiment in the general population.

NOTES

1   One cannot treat seriously an estimate of 5 million recently proferred by
     Dmitri Prokofiev, Israel Radio's Moscow correspondent. He cited a report
     from the "demographic centre of the Russian parliament" showing that "mil-
     lions of Jews are only now emerging after 70 years in the communist closet."
     Professor Ryvkina checked with eight of the leading demographers, ethnog-
     raphers and sociological experts on Jewish problems in Moscow, including
     one who is connected to the Russian parliament. None had ever heard of this
     report—or, for that matter, of the "demographic centre of the Russian parlia-
     ment". See *Canadian Jewish News*, 29 April 1993.
2   Zvi Gitelman, "Recent demographic and migratory trends among Soviet
     Jews: Implications for policy", *Post-Soviet Geography*, vol. 33, no. 3, 1992,
     142.
3   Mark Tolts, "Jewish marriages in the USSR: A demographic analysis", *East
     European Jewish Affairs*, vol. 22, no. 2, 1992, 9.
4   Mordechai Altshuler, *Soviet Jewry Since the Second World War: Population
     and Social Structure* (New York: Greenwood, 1987), 18-19, 22-3.
5   Sergio DellaPergolla, "The demographic context of the Soviet *aliya* [emigra-
     tion to Israel]", *Jews and Jewish Topics in the Soviet Union and Eastern
     Europe*, winter, 1991, 49-50.
6   See, for example, Stanley Lieberson and Mary Waters, "Ethnic groups in
     flux: The changing ethnic responses of American whites", *Annals of the
     American Academy of Social and Political Science*, no. 487, 1986, 79-91.
7   Recall that a third of the respondents who said they had changed their nation-
     ality registration switched *to* Jewish.
8   A study of emigrants headed to the West in the years 1976-79 found that
     over 19 per cent of them were non-Jews according to their passport registra-
     tion. However, many of them were spouses of Jews according to passport
     registration. See Victor Zaslavsky and Robert J. Brym, *Soviet-Jewish Emi-
     gration and Soviet Nationality Policy* (London: Macmillan, 1983), 52-5. As
     noted in the text, recent Israeli research found that the proportion of non-
     Jews by passport registration who emigrated to Israel was 5.8 per cent, al-
     though rising slightly over time. *Izvestiya* reported in 1990 that some 35 per
     cent of Soviet immigrants to Israel were Russians or members of other non-
     Jewish nationalities but I have seen no evidence to substantiate this claim.
     See G. F. Morozova, "Refugees and emigrants", *Sociological Research*, vol.
     32, no. 2, 1993, 93. In the light of these considerations, 15 per cent seems a
     credible estimate.
9   Sidney Heitman, "Jews in the 1989 USSR census", *Soviet Jewish Affairs*,
     vol. 20, no. 1, 1990, 23-30. Figures are rounded to the nearest thousand.
10   This is my calculation based on census figures. Altshuler, *Soviet Jewry . . .* ,
     30, 236 made comparable estimates before the results of the 1989 census
     were available.
11   Steven M. Cohen, *American Modernity and Jewish Identity* (New York and
     London: Tavistock, 1983).

36 *The Jews of Moscow, Kiev and Minsk*

12   The North American data are from Jay Brodbar-Nemzer *et al.*, "An over-
      view of the Canadian Jewish community" in Robert J. Brym, William
      Shaffir and Morton Weinfeld (eds.), *The Jews in Canada* (Toronto: Oxford
      University Press, 1993), 43, 46, 48, 61. Question-wording varied in the sur-
      veys. The Canadian figure for mixed marriage is for Toronto only but earlier
      studies have shown that Toronto is extremely close to the national figure.

13   Zvi Gitelman, "The evolution of Jewish culture and identity in the Soviet
      Union" in Yaacov Ro'i and Avi Beker (eds.), *Jewish Culture and Identity in
      the Soviet Union* (New York and London: New York University Press,
      1991), 8.

14   Richard Pipes, "The Soviet Union adrift", *Foreign Affairs*, vol. 70, no. 1,
      1991, 80.

15   All statistical analysis was conducted using SPSS-PC version 4.0. I first sub-
      stituted missing values on all 22 items with the means of those items. I then
      standardized the 22 items and ran a reliability test. The test revealed that
      items 70 and 62 scaled poorly with the other items. They were therefore
      dropped from the scale. The remaining 20 items yielded a healthy
      Cronbach's-alpha reliability coefficient of 0.804. I added up the standard-
      ized scores of the 20 items to create the index of Jewishness. The range of
      the scale is from -37.25 to 14.63, with low negative scores indicating high
      levels of Jewishness. For greater intuitive appeal, the trichotomized version
      of the scale was coded so that a high score indicates a high level of
      Jewishness.

16   Zvi Gitelman, "The evolution . . . ", 7-8. Research based on random samples
      of American Jews has also failed to find any such relationship. See Steven
      M. Cohen, 82-3.

17   Specifically, chi-square is not large enough to allow me to reject the hypoth-
      esis at the .05 probability level that the distribution of Jewishness by educa-
      tional level is due to chance (chi-square = 17.38, d.f. = 10, sig. = .07).

18   It is highly likely that there exists a reciprocal relationship between
      Jewishness and emigration plans—each contributes to causing the other—
      but in order to keep my presentation straightforward I will not attempt to
      construct a structural equation model that reflects such complex causal rela-
      tions.

19   Steven Erlanger, "As Ukraine loses Jews, the Jews lose a tradition", *The
      New York Times*, 27 August 1992.

20   Jean-Paul Sartre, *Anti-Semite and Jew*, trans. George J. Becker (New York:
      Schocken, 1965 [1948]), 143.

21   Jonathan Frankel, "The Soviet regime and anti-Zionism: An analysis" in
      Ro'i and Beker, 348-9; Ludmilla Tsigelman, "The impact of ideological
      changes in the USSR on different generations of the Soviet Jewish intelli-
      gentsia" in Ro'i and Beker, 70.

22   Michael Hechter, "Group formation and the cultural division of labor", *Ame-
      rican Journal of Sociology*, vol. 84, 1978, 293-318.

23   Here and throughout the book I use the stepwise regression technique.
      At each step in this procedure, the independent variable not in the equa-
      tion which has the smallest probability of F is entered if that probability is
      sufficiently small. SPSS-PC default values are retained. In order to keep my

1 Hebrew class in Minsk (with picture of Lenin still hanging on wall).

2 Lone Jew in front of Babi Yar holocaust memorial, near Kiev, Ukraine.

presentation simple I do not consider whether variables not included in the final equation have indirect effects.

24 A hugely disproportionate number of the leaders of the Jewish community in the region are men. These results suggest, however, that Jewish mothers are the unrecognized heroines of the community, playing nearly twice as important a role as Jewish fathers in causing respondents to develop Jewish identities, beliefs and patterns of practice.

4 Antisemitism

ANTISEMITISM AS A REACTION TO POST-COMMUNISM[1]

Imagine a country in which only 12 per cent of the adult population are satisfied with their lives, 71 per cent find it a financial strain even to clothe their families, 61 per cent report a deterioration in living standards over the past three months, 67 per cent report a decline in the political situation over the same period, and 41 per cent think that the country runs a high risk of complete anarchy. In the same country, only 13 per cent of adults trust the head of state—3 per cent fewer than distrust him—while 71 per cent express little or no trust in the parliament and 57 per cent express little or no trust in the government. Meanwhile, a mere 2 per cent of the adult population belong to a political party or movement and 53 per cent believe that mass disturbances, anti-government riots and bloodshed are likely to break out. That was the situation in Russia in March 1993 according to a country-wide public opinion poll of 2,000 people conducted by the Institute of Sociology of the Russian Academy of Sciences.[2] The poll and others like it show that in Russia, Ukraine and Belarus there is widespread despair, pessimism and political mistrust but no widely perceived economic and political alternative to the status quo. It also suggests potential danger. As Václav Havel recently put it:

> In a situation where one system has collapsed and a new one does not yet exist, many people feel empty and frustrated. This condition is fertile ground for radicalism of all kinds, for the hunt for scapegoats, and for the need to hide behind the anonymity of a group, be it socially or ethnically based. . . . It gives rise to the search for a common and easily identifiable enemy, to political extremism. . . .[3]

Or in the words of Nikolai Popov, one of Russia's leading public opinion pollsters, "people . . . seem ready to support political demagogues or opportunists . . . who promise the quick salvation of the country, and a way out of the economic chaos."[4]

38

In this volatile context the question of antisemitism—its level, social distribution, and possible political uses—takes on special significance. Antisemites have often blamed Jews for the ills of their societies. The former Soviet Union has a long tradition of antisemitism and the largest combined number of Jews and people with negative attitudes towards Jews of any region in the world. The potential for casting Jews in their traditional role of scapegoat thus appears large.

ANTISEMITISM AND PUBLIC OPINION POLLS

Despite the obvious significance of the subject, survey data on antisemitism in the region are meagre. In a 1991 overview of the subject, Gitelman was able to cite only two survey-based studies.[5] The first study reviews the results of a December 1988 telephone poll of 1,006 randomly-selected Muscovites and an April 1989 telephone poll of 1,000 randomly-selected Muscovites.[6] These polls provide evidence that people with negative attitudes towards Jews tend to be older, less educated people with lower socioeconomic status who share various anti-Western, authoritarian and Russian nationalist opinions. They suggest that people who give "undecided" responses tend to be "closet" antisemites. On that basis it was concluded that about a third of Muscovites hold a set of beliefs that include negative attitudes towards Jews.

The second study was conducted in February-March 1990. It was based on a small random sample of 504 Muscovites. The researchers asked respondents numerous questions about their attitudes towards Jews during in-home, face-to-face surveys. They concluded that negative attitudes towards Jews were concentrated among less educated people whose financial condition was deteriorating and who opposed democratization. However, the level of antisemitism discovered by the researchers was less than they expected, probably because they arbitrarily decided that the large number of "uncertain" responses necessarily indicated neutrality rather than a cover-up of negative attitudes.[7]

Since Gitelman's article was written, the results of a third study of antisemitism in the former Soviet Union have been published. L. D. Gudkov and A. G. Levinson conducted a large survey of nearly 8,000 randomly-selected people in Russia, Ukraine, Belarus, Latvia, Lithuania, Estonia, Moldova, Azerbaydzhan, Georgia, Kazakhstan and Uzbekistan under the auspices of VTsIOM, the Moscow-based All-Russian Centre for Public Opinion Research, in October 1990 and March 1992.[8] They asked a wide range of questions concerning respondents' attitudes towards Jews. The authors judged that in these republics a "feeling of tolerance [towards Jews] remains predominant."[9] Because the findings I am about to report lead me to quite different conclusions, I will discuss the Gudkov-Levinson survey in detail in the context of my own data analysis below.

Between 9 and 11 October 1992 I conducted a brief telephone poll in Moscow with the assistance of Professor Andrei Degtyarev of the Department of Political Science and Sociology of Politics at Moscow State University. The poll consisted of seventeen questions, two of which dealt with Jews. The interviewers had one to one-and-a-half years of interview training and experience. The survey was based on a randomly generated list of 1,060 residential telephone numbers in metropolitan Moscow. Interviews were completed with 989 respondents, yielding a very high 93 per cent response rate. Once Jews and respondents under eighteen years of age were deleted from the data set, 946 respondents remained. They are the respondents I analyze here. The maximum margin of error for a sample of this size is ±3.2 per cent, nineteen times out of twenty.

Telephone polls in Moscow are able to tap the opinions of just over three-quarters of the population. The rest have no telephones in their places of residence. Young couples, people living in recently constructed buildings and recently settled neighbourhoods, migrant workers and refugees are necessarily underrepresented in telephone surveys. Individuals living in communal apartments are also less likely than people living in single-family apartments to be interviewed in a telephone poll because many residents share a single telephone in communal apartments and only one respondent per telephone was allowed. These factors introduce unknown biases in estimates of distributions. In order to control for some of those unknown biases, I weighted the sample to match the age and gender distributions of the Moscow population according to the 1989 census. Strictly speaking, however, findings about the proportion of people expressing an attitude should be understood to apply only to people with telephones in their places of residence. On the other hand, sample bias does not usually affect relationships among variables: one may be reasonably confident that the relationship found between, say, income and antisemitism is accurate within sampling error.

Before reporting the results of the survey I must emphasize three points that will help place the findings in social context. First, when I discuss antisemitism I refer only to negative attitudes towards Jews, not to a highly articulated ideological system. There are some Muscovites who are antisemites in the strict ideological sense, people for whom anti-Jewish beliefs constitute a worldview. Such people represent only a small minority of the city's population. A much larger proportion simply hold negative attitudes towards Jews, as we will see. Second, although negative attitudes towards Jews are widespread in Moscow, contradictory trends are also evident. Among some categories of the population tolerance towards Jews is growing. Nonetheless, the data show that negative attitudes towards Jews are common. Finally, Jews are not the most disliked ethnic group in Moscow. A survey of 1,009 Muscovites conducted at the end of 1992 showed that various groups of so-called *chernye* (blacks) are least liked. Azeris are the most disliked ethnic group in Moscow, followed by Chechens, Gypsies, Georgians, and Armenians. Jews rank above the *chernye*—but well below Slavic groups such as Ukrainians.[10]

THE FREQUENCY OF ANTISEMITIC ATTITUDES IN MOSCOW

With these qualifications in mind, I begin by reporting the distribution of responses to a question regarding belief in the existence of a global plot against Russia organized by "Zionists" (i.e. Jews). The myth of an international Jewish conspiracy as manifested in the Tsarist secret police forgery *The Protocols of the Elders of Zion* has become an established element in the ideological makeup of hardcore antisemites the world over. Hardcore antisemites constituted roughly 3 per cent of the US population in 1981 and 4 per cent of the Canadian population outside Quebec in 1984.[11] If, in the Russian context, one is prepared to view hardcore antisemites as people who are inclined to agree that an international Jewish (or "Zionist") plot against Russia exists, then Table 4.1 suggests that the corresponding figure in Moscow is much higher—and Moscow, it must be remembered, is among the more liberal areas of Russia.[12] Specifically, 18 per cent of the respondents agreed or were inclined to agree that a global "Zionist" plot against Russia exists. Of course, the atmosphere of rapid economic decline and political instability that characterizes Russia today is a natural breeding ground for conspiracy theories. Many such theories coexist, and belief in a "Zionist" plot is not necessarily the most widespread of them.[13] Our respondents may have been reacting to the word "plot" as much as to the word "Zionist". That said, the proportion of Muscovites open to the possibility that a "Zionist" plot is responsible for Russia's predicament is very high by North American standards.

Nearly a quarter of the respondents said that they were "undecided" as to whether a "Zionist" plot against Russia existed. Do such responses

Table 4.1
*"Do you believe that there is a global plot against
Russia organized by 'Zionists'?"*

	frequency	per cent
yes	128	14
inclined to agree	39	4
undecided	229	24
inclined to disagree	53	6
no	492	52
total	940	100

indicate real indecision and neutrality or do they mask the attitudes of
antisemites who simply do not want to express their opinions openly?
The answer to this question is critically important. If the "undecideds" are
in fact antisemites, then one is entitled to reach the shocking conclusion that negative attitudes towards Jews engulf more than 40 per cent of
Muscovites.

Table 4.2 suggests that such an alarming conclusion is *not* warranted.
Respondents were asked whether they preferred the old or new political
order and whether they held the West responsible for Russia's crisis. For
both items clearly reactionary responses were possible. I reasoned that if
the "undecideds" on the "Zionist" plot question tended to prefer the old
political order and held the West responsible for Russia's crisis at least as
much as did those who expressed belief in the existence of a "Zionist" plot,
then that would constitute evidence for the view that the "undecideds" are
in fact closet antisemites. As Table 4.2 shows, however, the percentage
of those who prefer the old order and of those who blame the West for
Russia's crisis both decline smoothly as one moves horizontally across Table 4.2 from the "yes" to the "no" column, with "undecided" squarely in
between.

Although the "undecideds" really do appear to be a neutral category
between "yes" and "no", one should bear in mind the substantive meaning
of my finding. Nearly a quarter of adult Muscovites are undecided on the
question of whether there exists an international "Zionist" conspiracy.

Table 4.2
Belief in Global "Zionist" Plot against Russia by Reactionary Attitudes
(in per cent; n in parentheses)

	belief in global plot				
	yes	inclined to yes	undecided	inclined to no	no
political preference					
old	58	53	45	26	25
other	42	47	55	74	75
total	100 (119)	100 (32)	100 (199)	100 (47)	100 (448)
West responsible					
yes	70	46	21	10	7
other	30	54	79	90	93
total	100 (128)	100 (39)	100 (229)	100 (53)	100 (492)

Together with the fact that nearly 18 per cent of the city's adult population have decided that such a conspiracy *is* probably afoot, it suggests that over 40 per cent of Moscow's adult population are open to this antisemitic canard.

The respondents were asked a second question about Jews—whether they had ever witnessed an infringement of Jewish rights. Table 4.3 sets out the responses to that question. Perhaps surprisingly, fewer than a fifth of the respondents said they had witnessed such an infringement; over three-quarters denied they had, and nearly five per cent were undecided. Here again we are confronted with a quandary: do the "never" and "undecided" responses indicate genuine ignorance of discrimination against Jews? Or do they suggest a refusal to view Jews as victims since Jews, as every antisemite knows, can only be advantaged. The evidence favours the latter interpretation, as Table 4.4 makes clear. Those who claim never to have witnessed an infringement of Jewish rights or to be undecided on the issue are more likely than others to believe in the existence of a global

Table 4.3
"Have you ever witnessed an infringement of the rights of Jews?"

	frequency	per cent
often	69	7
sometimes	114	12
never	712	76
undecided	45	5
total	940	100

Table 4.4
Witnessing Infringement of Rights of Jews by Reactionary Attitudes
(in per cent; n in parentheses)

| | infringement of rights | | |
	often	sometimes	never
global plot			
yes	16	18	19
don't know	14	10	26
no	70	73	56
total	100 (69)	101 (114)	101 (711)
political preference			
old	23	26	37
other	77	74	63
total	100 (62)	100 (108)	100 (632)
West responsible			
yes	14	17	20
other	86	83	80
total	100 (69)	100 (114)	100 (712)

Note: Percentages do not necessarily add up to 100 due to rounding.

"Zionist" plot against Russia, to prefer the old political order, and to believe that the West is responsible for Russia's crisis. The fact that over 80 per cent of Muscovites claim ignorance of any violation of Jewish rights cannot therefore be taken as an indication of the absence of such violations since many of these people adhere to a set of reactionary ideas that includes negative attitudes towards Jews.

ANTISEMITIC ATTITUDES IN THE CIS

How can I reconcile my more dismal conclusion with the view of Gudkov and Levinson, noted above, that tolerance towards Jews predominates in Russia and other republics of the former Soviet Union? Quite easily: my standard of comparison apparently differs from theirs. Consider some of Gudkov's and Levinson's findings, reproduced in Table 4.5. The percentage of respondents who expressed negative attitudes towards Jews varies by attitude and by republic. By North American standards, however, all the proportions are large. For example, depending on republic, between 34 and 68 per cent of Gudkov and Levinson's respondents opposed Jews marrying into their families. Polls conducted in the USA in 1981 and in Canada in 1984 show that the comparable figure for both North American countries was only 10 per cent. In Canada 21 per cent of respondents opposed blacks marrying whites; in the USA the figure was 33 per cent.[14] Thus Gudkov's and Levinson's data convince me that there is considerably more opposition to Jewish-non-Jewish intermarriage in the former Soviet Union than there is opposition to black-white intermarriage in the USA. In general, the percentages in Table 4.5 portray a level of animosity against Jews that exceeds black-white animosities in the USA. Gudkov and Levinson are entitled to regard this as "tolerance", but most North Americans employ a different vocabulary to describe such a situation.[15]

Figure 4.1 uses an unpublished republic-by-republic breakdown of the fourteen questions in Table 4.5 to construct a graph of the incidence of antisemitism by republic. It shows the average percentage of respondents in each republic who gave negative responses to Gudkov's and Levinson's fourteen questions about Jews in 1992. (Georgia was not polled in the 1992 wave of their study.) Of most interest here are the relative positions of Russia, Ukraine and Belarus. While Russia and Ukraine rank near the bottom of the scale, Belarus ranks near the top. If I concluded on the basis of the Moscow telephone survey that antisemitic attitudes are wide-

Table 4.5
Attitudes Towards Jews in Ten Soviet Republics, March 1992 (in per cent)

percentage of respondents who . . .	range	mean
do not approve of Jews as workers	33-55	44.0
are unwilling to work in the same group with Jews	23-38	30.5
maintain that Jews avoid physical work	65-75	70.0
maintain that Jews value making money and profit above human relations	40-53	46.5
are not willing to have a Jew as their immediate boss at work	47-57	52.0
think it is necessary to limit the number of Jews in leading positions	19-33	26.0
are reluctant to see a Jew as president of their republic	53-76	64.5
maintain that Jews do not make good family men	35-56	45.5
have non-positive perceptions of neighbourliness of Jewish families	26-48	37.0
are unwilling to have Jews as members of one's family	34-68	51.0
do not support equal opportunity for ethnic group members to obtain work	17-35	26.0
do not support equal opportunity for ethnic group members to attend educational institutions	15-34	24.5
often have negative feelings towards Jewish parties and organizations	25-45	35.0

Source: Adapted from L. D. Gudkov and A. G. Levinson, "Attitudes towards Jews", *Sotsiologicheskiye issledovaniya*, no. 12, 1992, 109.

Note: Scores for each republic were not reported by the authors. Thus in calculating the mean, republics could not be weighted for population size.

spread in that relatively liberal city, one is obliged to conclude from the Gudkov and Levinson survey that the situation is even more dire in Belarus and most of the rest of the former USSR.

Figure 4.1
Level of Antisemitism in Ten Former Soviet Republics, 1992 (in per cent)

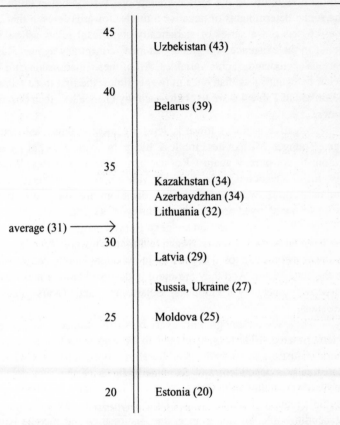

45

Uzbekistan (43)

40

Belarus (39)

35

Kazakhstan (34)
Azerbaydzhan (34)
Lithuania (32)

average (31) ⎯⎯⎯→
30

Latvia (29)

Russia, Ukraine (27)

25   Moldova (25)

20   Estonia (20)

Source: Gudkov and Levinson, unpublished data.

Note: This figure shows the mean per cent of respondents who gave negative responses to fourteen questionnaire items concerning Jews. The overall average is based on republic means, not individual scores.

THE SOCIAL DETERMINANTS OF ANTISEMITISM

Let us now return to the Moscow telephone survey and examine some of the social determinants of negative attitudes towards Jews in that city. Table 4.6 sets out a series of statistically significant relationships between belief in the existence of a global "Zionist" conspiracy against Russia and various sociodemographic variables. All of these relationships are likely to occur by chance less than once in twenty times; the first three relationships described in Table 4.6 are likely to occur by chance less than once in 1,000 times.

Negative attitudes towards Jews are most strongly associated with age. Younger Muscovites are less likely to express belief in a global "Zionist" conspiracy against Russia than older Muscovites. Work status also influences belief in this issue. Private employers, students, and white-collar workers with a university education are the least antisemitic groups. Unemployed people, blue-collar workers, and white-collar workers with middle-school education are next. Retired people and homemakers are the most antisemitic groups. Negative attitudes towards Jews also increase in lower income groups. They are more prevalent among people who work in the state sector. And they are more widespread among non-Russians in Moscow—especially Ukrainians, Belarusians, and Tatars—than among Russians.

The socio-demographic variables mentioned are themselves intercorrelated. Elderly people tend to be less educated, have particular work statuses, and so forth. It is therefore important to ask what are the statistically independent and combined effects of the sociodemographic variables on belief in a global "Zionist" conspiracy against Russia. The multiple regression analysis reported in Table 4.7 answers that question. In descending order of importance, age, nationality and income have independent effects on antisemitic belief.[16]

Belief in the existence of a global "Zionist" conspiracy against Russia is also correlated with other attitudes, as can be seen in Table 4.8. All of the relationships reported in Table 4.8 are likely to occur by chance less than once in 1,000 times. We already know that Muscovites with negative attitudes towards Jews are more inclined to believe that the West is responsible for the crisis in Russia, to prefer the old political system, and to deny witnessing any infringements of Jewish rights. Table 4.8 also demonstrates that people with negative attitudes towards Jews are more likely to expect living conditions to be the same or worse in five years. Moreover, and somewhat ominously, people with negative attitudes towards Jews are

Table 4.6
Socio-demographic Correlates of Belief in Global "Zionist" Conspiracy against Russia (in per cent; n in parentheses)

	belief in "Zionist" conspiracy		
	yes; inclined to think so; undecided	inclined to think not; no	total
age			
<31	32	68	100 (232)
31-59	38	62	100 (490)
60+	61	39	100 (218)
chi-square = 46.47, d.f. = 2, p<.001; tau-c = -0.213			
work status			
employer, student, white collar/ univ	32	68	100 (361)
unemployed, worker white collar/ middle	43	57	100 (333)
retired/ homemaker	56	44	100 (246)
chi-square = 34.64, d.f. = 2, p<.001; tau-c = -0.204			
monthly income in roubles			
<3,000	50	50	100 (450)
3,000-10,000	36	64	100 (395)
>10,000	32	68	100 (95)
chi-square = 20.73, d.f. = 2, p<.001; tau-c = 0.152			
sector of employment			
state	42	58	100 (443)
mixed	29	71	100 (41)
private	29	71	100 (129)
chi-square = 8.46, d.f. = 2, p<.025; tau-c = 0.104			
gender			
male	38	62	100 (402)
female	45	55	100 (538)
chi-square = 5.46, d.f. = 2, p<.05; tau-c = -0.074			
nationality			
Russian	40	60	100 (826)
other	49	51	100 (35)
Ukr/Bel/Tat	59	41	101 (78)
chi-square = 11.12, d.f. = 2, p<.005; tau-c = -0.067			

Note: Percentages do not necessarily add up to 100 due to rounding.

somewhat more likely than people with positive attitudes towards Jews to express willingness to protest their dissatisfaction openly by taking part in strikes, demonstrations, boycotts and even by destroying property. Specifically, among people who are prepared to protest actively their dissatisfaction with declining living conditions, 53 per cent believe in, or are undecided about, the existence of a global "Zionist" conspiracy against Russia, while 47 per cent are inclined to deny the existence of such a plot. In contrast, among those who are *not* prepared to protest declining living conditions openly, 35 per cent believe in, or are undecided about, the existence of a "Zionist" conspiracy and 65 per cent are inclined to deny the existence of such a plot.

Table 4.7

Multiple Regression of Belief in Global "Zionist" Conspiracy against Russia on Sociodemographic Variables (weighted results)

variable	slope (b)	standard error	standardized slope (beta)	t
age	-0.27	0.04	-0.20	-6.09
Russian/ other	0.50	0.14	0.11	3.54
income	0.14	0.06	0.07	2.09

intercept = 4.04; n = 938; adjusted R^2 = .06

The multiple regression analysis summarized in Table 4.9 may be interpreted to suggest the "distance" between belief in a global "Zionist" conspiracy against Russia and various attitudes that are independently and statistically significantly related to that belief at the .05 probability level. Blaming the West for Russia's ills is very strongly associated with belief in a "Zionist" conspiracy. In addition, preference for the pre-Gorbachev political order and belief that women's proper role is in the home rather than in the paid labour force are significantly and independently associated with belief in the conspiracy theory.[17] The evidence thus suggests that some large categories of Moscow's population hold attitudes that are authoritarian, xenophobic, illiberal on social issues and, of course, antisemitic.[18] Given the prevalence of negative attitudes towards Jews in the city, and the even greater prevalence of negative attitudes towards Jews elsewhere in the former USSR, the Jews of the region have reason to be anxious.

Table 4.8
Attitudinal Correlates of Belief in Global "Zionist" Conspiracy against Russia (in per cent; n in parentheses)

	belief in "Zionist" conspiracy		
	yes; inclined to think so; undecided	inclined to think not; no	total
West responsible for Russian crisis			
yes	68	32	100 (426)
no	21	79	100 (515)
chi-square = 216.66, d.f. = 1, p<.001; tau-c = 0.471			
political preference			
old system	55	45	100 (455)
new system	26	74	100 (390)
chi-square = 74.30, d.f. = 1, p<.001; tau-c = 0.291			
expected living conditions in 5 years			
same/worse	47	54	101 (401)
better	30	70	100 (242)
chi-square = 19.09, d.f. = 1, p<.001; tau-c = -0.161			
protest if living conditions worsen			
yes	53	47	100 (215)
no	35	65	100 (560)
chi-square = 25.85, d.f. = 1, p<.001; tau-c = -0.161			
witnessed infringement of rights of Jews			
often/ sometimes	28	72	100 (183)
undecided/ never	46	54	100 (755)
chi-square = 18.65, d.f. = 1, p<.001; tau-c = -0.111			

Note: Percentages do not necessarily add up to 100 due to rounding.

Table 4.9
Multiple Regression of Belief in Global "Zionist" Conspiracy
against Russia on Attitudinal Variables

variable	slope (b)	standard error	standardized slope (beta)	t
West responsible	0.46	0.03	0.52	16.72
political preference	0.17	0.05	0.11	3.36
women's role	0.19	0.08	0.07	2.37

intercept= 1.49; n = 794; adjusted R^2 = 0.33

JEWISH PERCEPTIONS OF ANTISEMITISM

The survey of Jews in Moscow, Kiev and Minsk asked a battery of questions concerning perceptions of antisemitism. Not surprisingly in light of the findings summarized above, over 95 per cent of Jews responded "yes" when asked if they believed that antisemitism existed in their country.

Those who answered "yes" were also asked "What are the main manifestations of antisemitism in your country today?" Interviewers did not prompt respondents with a list of possible answers; they could reply in any way they wished. Respondents were, however, asked to rank their replies, that is, to state their opinion of the main manifestation of antisemitism, the second most important manifestation and so forth. Table 4.10 sets out their first choices.

Table 4.10
Jewish Perceptions of Main Forms of Antisemitism (first choice in per cent)

	frequency	per cent
q118-people hostile	326	38
q119-nationalist organizations	212	25
q117-state policy	197	23
q120-articles in press	84	10
q121-people envious	40	5
total	859	100

Nearly 40 per cent of the respondents regard hostility on the part of ordinary people as the main source of antisemitism in their country today. A quarter of them think that the main source of antisemitism lies in the threat of nationalist organizations such as Pamyat and Otechestvo. About the same proportion view state policy as the main source of antisemitism. A tenth of the respondents perceive the nationalist press—publications such as *Molodaya gvardiya* and *Literaturnaya Rossiya*—as the chief manifestation of anti-Jewish feeling. And 5 per cent of them mention popular envy as the most important source of antisemitism in their country today.[19]

The only real surprise here concerns state policy. Russia, Ukraine and Belarus no longer have a state-sponsored policy of discrimination against Jews. That nearly a quarter of the Jews in the three cities nonetheless believe the state to be the main locus of anti-Jewish discrimination probably indicates a combination of three things. First, some individual state officials presumably continue to discriminate against Jews in employment and in other spheres of life despite the abandonment of state-backed antisemitism. Second, since historical memories die hard, some Jews who feel disadvantaged are likely to attribute some or all of their disabilities to their Jewish origin, whether or not this is objectively justifiable. Blaming state authorities for blocking their mobility and making their professional lives unsatisfying is probably a sort of historical reflex for some Jews. Third, in all three cities, and in Moscow in particular, mass anti-Jewish demonstrations are held, antisemitic signs are posted and an active nationalist-fascist press publishes articles and cartoons worthy of *Der Stürmer*. The Ukrainian and, especially, Russian and Belarusian states do little to combat these openly antisemitic acts. Reluctance to put active antisemites out of business by passing tough laws banning the propagation of ethnic hatred and enforcing those laws by means of a police crackdown is perhaps viewed by some Jews as a form of state antisemitism. Just how important each of these three factors is cannot, however, be ascertained on the basis of the available data.

Examining city-to-city variations reveals that antisemitism is perceived differently and takes different forms in different places. Consider Figure 4.2. It shows the proportion of respondents in each city who (1) believe that antisemitism exists; (2) fear antisemitism very much; (3) say they feared antisemitism very much six or seven years ago; (4) feel that pogroms are likely or certain to break out; and (5) have personally experienced antisemitism. Notice that about 5 per cent more Muscovites than Kievans and Minskers believe that antisemitism exists. Roughly 15 per cent more Muscovites than Kievans and Minskers believe that pogroms are likely or certain to break out. And approximately a third more Muscovites than Kievans and Minskers say they feared antisemitism very much six or seven years ago.

It would, however, be mistaken to conclude on the basis of this last batch of figures that Moscow is a more antisemitic city than Kiev and Minsk. After all, Figure 4.2 also shows that the proportion of Moscow Jews who fear antisemitism very much has been cut by more than half since the advent of Gorbachev so that today there is no inter-city difference in the level of fear. In addition, about 10 per cent more Minskers than Muscovites and Kievans have actually experienced antisemitism personally.

Why should more Moscow Jews feel that antisemitism exists and that they are likely to be attacked? Why should they hold such opinions despite experiencing by far the largest drop in fear of antisemitism and personally experiencing substantially less antisemitism than Minsk Jews? Figures 4.3 helps solve this puzzle. It shows the proportion of respondents in each city who ranked each form of antisemitism first. The Moscow profile is strikingly different from that of the other two cities. Moscow Jews are much

Figure 4.2
Perceptions of Antisemitism by City (in per cent)

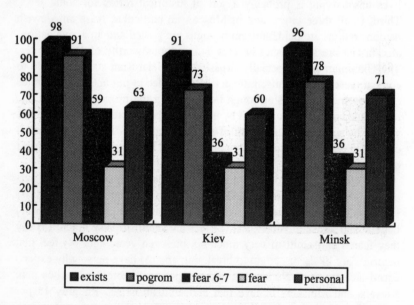

more likely than Jews from Kiev and Minsk to believe that the main manifestation of antisemitism may be found in the activities of nationalist organizations and the nationalist press. That is undoubtedly because Moscow
has a more active anti-Jewish press and larger and better-organized anti-
Jewish organizations than Kiev and Minsk. Thus between August 1991 and
August 1992 antisemitic materials appeared in twenty-two newspapers and
five journals published in Moscow. Some of this material is exported to
Kiev and Minsk, where antisemitic literature is produced on a far smaller
scale.[20] The hysterical nationalist press makes Moscow Jews feel that antisemitism is more widespread in their country. Rabidly nationalist organizations make Moscow Jews feel that they are more open to attack. If Moscow
Jews have nonetheless experienced the greatest decline in fear of antisemitism over the past six or seven years, that may be attributed to the
cessation of anti-Jewish activities on the part of the Russian state. Moscow
is no longer the font of state-backed antisemitism, as it was in the pre-
Gorbachev years. That has clearly brought most relief to the Jews located
closest to the source of the problem.

Figure 4.3
Forms of Antisemitism by City (first choice in per cent)

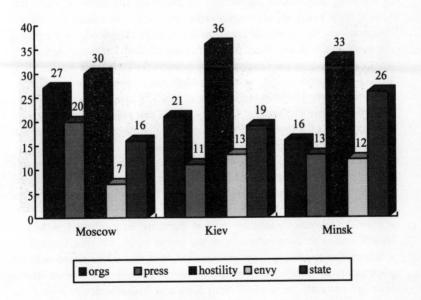

If Moscow ranks first in the perception of what might be called organized group antisemitism then the view is most widespread in Minsk that
antisemitism still resides chiefly in state practice. Over a quarter of Minsk
Jews hold that opinion compared to fewer than a fifth of Kiev Jews and a
sixth of Moscow Jews. Finally, Kiev ranks significantly ahead of the other
two cities in the perception that antisemitism is based mainly in the population at large. Some 49 per cent of Kiev Jews think that the main locus of
antisemitism lies in popular hostility towards, and envy of, Jews, compared
to 45 per cent of Minsk Jews and 37 per cent of Moscow Jews.

I conclude that one cannot properly speak of a given locale being
simply more or less antisemitic than another. Antisemitism is multi-dimen-
sional, taking different forms in different places.[21] To be sure, popular hostility towards, and envy of, Jews is perceived as the main source of antisemitism in Moscow, Kiev *and* Minsk. To that degree, educational and
inter-communal programmes aimed at enlightening and liberalizing non-
Jews are desperately needed in all three cities. But it is also evident that a
distinctive policy mix is required to combat antisemitism in different cities.

In Kiev the government and the leading opposition movement, *Rukh*,
have been most effective in combatting the organized-group and official
forms of antisemitism. They have also taken meaningful steps to re-educate
the public. For example, in 1991 officials participated in ceremonies com-
memorating the fiftieth anniversary of the Nazi massacre of Ukrainian
Jews at Babi Yar. They also organized a series of public events, including a
memorial service in which President Kravchuk acknowledged the partial
responsibility of Ukrainians for the massacre. Such measures apparently
work: according to the Gudkov and Levinson poll, Ukraine was the only
area of the former USSR apart from Moldova to experience a decline in
hostility towards Jews between 1990 and 1992.[22] History, however, is long.
According to my survey data, Kiev Jews think that popular hostility against
them is more of a problem than do Jews in the other two cities. Popular
education is still needed in Kiev more than elsewhere.

We learned from Figure 4.1 that Belarus suffers from a considerably
higher level of popular antisemitism than either Ukraine or Russia. Indeed,
the Gudkov and Levinson survey shows that Belarus registered one of the
largest *increases* in antisemitic feeling in the former USSR between 1990
and 1992.[23] Popular education cannot therefore be neglected in Minsk.
However, it is perhaps indicative of the higher level of residual state antisemitism that the Belarus government has been much less active than the
government of Ukraine in re-educating its citizenry about the Jews. Minsk
Jews are certainly more likely than Kiev and Moscow Jews to view the

Belarusian state as still rife with antisemites. Therefore, a thorough housecleaning of antisemitic officials seems more needed in Minsk than in the other two cities.

Between 1990 and 1992 the level of antisemitic hostility among Russia's population remained just about constant. In Moscow, however, group antisemitism is especially prominent. There, political control of highly active and organized antisemitic Russian nationalists is needed more than in Kiev and Minsk.

SOCIODEMOGRAPHIC VARIATIONS

Fear is the only dimension of antisemitism in Figure 4.2 that does not vary from city to city: in Moscow, Kiev and Minsk, 31 per cent of Jews express a great deal of apprehension about antisemitism. Let us now examine the social bases of their fear.[24]

Table 4.11 establishes that a host of factors are related to fear of antisemitism on the part of Jews. These factors fall into four groups:

- First are what might be called vulnerability factors. Jews who are most frightened of antisemitism tend to be middle-aged, female and employed in white-collar jobs the security of which is no longer assured now that the market is beginning to take slow root and the huge government bureaucracy is being inexorably cut back. They also tend to have a low standard of living and earn low incomes.[25] Indeed, the people with the highest unemployment rate in the general population share many of these characteristics.[26] So far at least, manual workers, government administrators and people who own or manage private businesses—"others" in the crude occupational breakdown of Table 4.11—tend not to be threatened as much by unemployment, especially if they are men.[27]

- Second are factors indicating dissatisfaction with one's economic prospects. Fear of antisemitism is associated with discontent concerning income and opportunities for upward mobility, with low expectations concerning one's standard of living in one to two years and with a general lack of confidence in one's future.

- Third are actual experiences of antisemitism. Fear of antisemitism is related to claiming that one witnessed antisemitism during the past year in one's place of work, in one's neighbourhood, in the mass media and in state policy.

Table 4.11
Fear of Antisemitism by Correlates (in per cent; n in parentheses)

| question | fear of antisemitism | | | |
	very	not very	not at all	total
q7-sex				
male	21	43	36	100 (483)
female	41	38	21	100 (469)
chi-square = 50.90, d.f. = 2, sig. = .000, tau-c = .247				
q8-age				
18-29	15	40	45	100 (170)
30-39	32	39	29	100 (142)
40-49	35	43	22	100 (205)
50-59	38	39	24	100 (277)
60-90	31	42	27	100 (159)
chi-square = 42.3, d.f. = 8, sig. = .000, tau-c = .125				
q17-occupation				
white collar	35	43	22	100 (403)
other	19	39	42	100 (217)
chi-square = 33.42, d.f. = 2, sig. = .000, tau-c = .234				
q20-income satisfaction				
satisfied	19	43	37	100 (172)
not satisfied	35	39	25	100 (428)
chi-square = 17.07, d.f. = 2, sig. = .000, tau-c = .162				
q25-opportunity satisfaction				
satisfied	27	39	35	100 (202)
not satisfied	36	43	21	100 (264)
chi-square = 11.85, d.f. = 2, sig. = .003, tau-c = .161				
q29-total income				
low	35	41	24	100 (287)
medium	32	45	23	100 (258)
high	27	38	36	100 (288)
chi-square = 15.64, d.f. = 4, sig. = .004, tau-c = .096				
q38-standard of living				
satisfied	24	36	40	100 (198)
not satisfied	35	41	25	100 (671)
chi-square = 19.34, d.f. = 2, sig. = .000, tau-c = .128				

Table 4.11 (cont'd)
Fear of Antisemitism by Correlates (in per cent; n in parentheses)

question	fear of antisemitism			
	very	not very	not at all	total
q39-expected standard of living				
better	20	36	45	100 (160)
same	28	47	25	100 (233)
worse	40	37	33	100 (372)
chi-square = 42.09, d.f. = 4, sig. = .000, tau-c = .178				
q41-upward mobility opportunities				
yes	22	37	41	100 (170)
no	35	41	24	100 (613)
chi-square = 20.71, d.f. = 2, sig. = .000, tau-c = .140				
q163-confidence in own future				
yes	18	31	51	100 (155)
no	38	41	21	100 (673)
chi-square = 62.26, d.f. = 2, sig. = .000, tau-c = .211				
q133-witness antisemitism at work				
none	25	41	34	100 (536)
little	44	37	20	100 (166)
lot	53	27	21	100 (42)
chi-square = 32.60, d.f. = 4, sig. = .000, tau-c = .146				
q134-witness antisemitism in neighbourhood				
none	29	40	31	100 (734)
little	37	43	20	100 (158)
lot	55	34	12	100 (38)
chi-square = 20.73, d.f. = 4, sig. = .000, tau-c = -.091				
q135-witness antisemitism in mass media				
none	20	32	48	100 (234)
little	29	48	24	100 (367)
lot	42	42	15	100 (300)
chi-square = 86.64, d.f. = 4, sig. = .000, tau-c = -.243				
q136-witness antisemitism in state policy				
none	26	40	35	100 (486)
little	35	45	20	100 (192)
lot	50	30	21	100 (104)
chi-square = 33.92, d.f. = 4, sig. = .000, tau-c = -.154				

Table 4.11 (cont'd)
Fear of Antisemitism by Correlates (in per cent; n in parentheses)

question	fear of antisemitism			
	very	not very	not at all	total
Jewishness scale				
high	42	39	19	100 (324)
medium	33	44	39	100 (311)
low	19	38	43	100 (318)
chi-square = 64.65, d.f. = 4, sig. = .000, tau-c = -.219				

▪ Last, fear of antisemitism is strongly related to strength of Jewishness: those with higher levels of Jewish identification and practice tend to fear antisemitism more. This suggests that the most Jewish Jews may be predisposed to perceive antisemitism and regard it as problematic.[28]

Table 4.12 reduces this long list of factors to only five variables that continue to exercise independent and statistically significant effects when entered into a regression equation. At least one variable comes from each of the four groups of factors isolated above. In short, middle-aged and less assimilated women who lack confidence in their own future are most likely to be frightened by antisemitism, particularly when they witness such outrages in the mass media.

Table 4.12
Multiple Regression of Fear of Antisemitism

question	slope (b)	standard error	standardized slope (beta)	t
q135-wit. media	.22	.03	.22	6.80
q7-sex	.34	.05	.22	6.87
Jewishness scale	.01	.003	.17	5.28
q163-conf. future	.35	.07	.17	5.38
q8-age	.08	.02	.14	4.54

intercept = 3.77; n = 786; adjusted R^2 = .217

SUMMARY

Not all Jews in Moscow, Kiev and Minsk regard antisemitism as a problem. Five per cent of them think that antisemitism does not even exist in their countries. A significant number of respondents think that it is *not* mainly nationalist groups and politicians who are behind the spread of antisemitism. Thus interviewers confronted respondents with the statement "The view is becoming widespread that antisemitism exists in your country. In your opinion, who has an interest in spreading this view?" Respondents were asked to rank their responses but they were not presented with a predetermined set of possible answers. Table 4.13 shows that a sixth of the respondents think that it is principally Jewish, Israeli and Western individuals and organizations who wish to spread the idea that antisemitism exists in their country. Finally, 29 per cent of the people in my sample say that they are "not at all" frightened of antisemitism.

Table 4.13
Parties Interested in Antisemitism (first choice in per cent)

question	frequency	per cent
q147-nationalist parties	326	43
q141-political opposition	141	19
q142-certain govt. officials	61	8
subtotal	528	70
q146-Israel, USA & oth. West.	41	5
q143-Jews in country	32	4
q144-Jew. orgs. from ex-USSR	29	4
q145-Jew. orgs. abroad	23	3
subtotal	125	17
q148-misc'l. other responses	98	13
total	751	100

All of these are minority opinions. The evidence assembled in this chapter demonstrates that the great majority of Jews recognize anti-semitism as a serious issue. The perceived dimensions of the problem vary by urban and national context. For example, Jews think that antisemitism is more an issue of popular hostility in Kiev than in Moscow and Minsk, more a problem of state policy in Minsk than in Kiev and Moscow, and more a question of organized anti-Jewish groups in Moscow than in Kiev and Minsk. But over 30 per cent of Jews in each city are very frightened of antisemitism and another 40 per cent are somewhat frightened. Particularly for women; people in their thirties, forties and fifties; less assimilated Jews; and those who regularly witness anti-Jewish excesses in the media, life is thus rendered extremely unsettling. In fact, as we will learn in the next chapter, the experience and fear of antisemitism are so intense and wide-spread that they are important factors prompting many Jews to want to leave their country.

This chapter also presents ample evidence that Jewish perceptions are solidly founded in reality. Many Russians and Ukrainians and propor-tionately even more Belarusians dislike Jews. Certainly the proportions in-volved are very considerably higher than in the West and amount to noth-ing like a situation of what Westerners commonly refer to as tolerance. This does not mean that many Jews are in imminent danger of being at-tacked by organized mobs or that the Slavic CIS states are systematically discriminating against Jews. On the other hand, as a group of Russian soci-ologists correctly concluded in a review of recent surveys, "there are no signs at the present that the influence of nationalist and ethnocentric ideas will diminish in the near future, and that consequently the significance and role of interethnic relations will decline as a factor in social tension."[29] Or as Arthur Hertzberg recently stated, the "recurrent fear everywhere in the former USSR is that the worsening economic situation might bring with it an anti-Semitism increasing to serious proportions."[30] As a result, most Jews in the region are in the historically familiar position of being caught between two worlds, feeling tremendous ambivalence about what, if any-thing, they should call home.

NOTES

1   This section is a revised version of Robert J. Brym and Andrei Degtyarev, "Anti-semitism in Moscow: Results of an October 1992 survey", *Slavic Review*, vol. 52, no. 1, 1993, 1-12.

2   A. Komozin (ed.), *Monitoring: The 1993 Russian Citizens' Opinion Poll Results* (Moscow: Institute of Sociology, Russian Academy of Sciences, 1993).

3   "The post-Communist nightmare," *The New York Review of Books*, 27 May 1993.

4   Nikolai P. Popov, "Political views of the Russian public", *The International Journal of Public Opinion Research*, vol. 4, no. 4, 1992, 330.

5   Zvi Gitelman, "Glasnost, perestroika and antisemitism", *Foreign Affairs*, vol. 70, no. 2, 1991, 155-6. A more detailed report on one of these studies was published after Gitelman's article was written. See James L. Gibson and Raymond M. Duch, "Anti-semitic attitudes of the mass public: Estimates and explanations based on a survey of the Moscow oblast", *Public Opinion Quarterly*, no. 56, 1992, 1-28. In addition, a few surveys of perceptions of antisemitism among Jewish community leaders in Russia and among Russian Jewish immigrants have been conducted. See Alexander Benifand, "Jewish emigration from the USSR in the 1990s" in Tanya Basok and Robert J. Brym (eds.), *Soviet-Jewish Emigration and Resettlement in the 1990s* (Toronto: York Lanes Press, York University, 1991), 38-41.

6   Gibson and Duch. I discuss this issue at greater length below.

7   Robert J. Brym, "*Perestroika*, public opinion, and *pamyat*", *Soviet Jewish Affairs*, vol. 19, no. 3, 1989, 23-32.

8   L. D. Gudkov and A. G. Levinson, "Attitudes towards Jews", *Sotsiologicheskiye issledovaniya*, no. 12, 1992, 108-11.

9   *Ibid.*, 111.

10 Vladimir Zotov, "The Chechen problem as seen by Muscovites", *Moskovsky komsomolets*, 12 January 1993.

11 Geraldine Rosenfield, "The polls: Attitudes toward American Jews", *Public Opinion Quarterly*, no. 46, 1982, 443; Robert J. Brym and Rhonda L. Lenton, "The distribution of antisemitism in Canada in 1984", *Canadian Journal of Sociology*, vol. 16, no. 4, 1991, 411-18. Here, hardcore anti-semites are defined as those scoring in the bottom 25 per cent of a scale indicating positive or negative feelings towards Jews. Eight per cent of Americans and 10 per cent of Canadians outside Quebec had negative feelings towards Jews, i.e., they scored in the bottom half of the scale. The American figures come from a 1981 Gallup poll. I calculated the Canadian figures from the 1984 Canadian National Election Study.

12 V. B. Koltsov and V. A. Mansurov, "Political ideologies in the *perestroyka* era", *Sotsiologicheskiye issledovaniya*, no. 10, 1991, 32 ; V. Yadov *et al.*, "The sociopolitical situation in Russia in mid-February 1992", *Sociological Research*, vol. 32, no. 2, 1993, 7; L. A. Sedov, "Yeltsin's rating", *Ekonomicheskiye i sotsialnye peremeny: monitoring obshchestvennogo mneniya*, Informatsionny byulleten, Intertsentr VTsIOM (Moscow: Aspekt Press, 1993), 15.

13   John F. Dunn, "Hard times in Russia foster conspiracy theories", Radio Free Europe/ Radio Liberty Special Report, 23 September 1992.

14   Ronald D. Lambert and James E. Curtis, *"Québécois* and English Canadian opposition to racial and religious intermarriage, 1968-1983", *Canadian Ethnic Studies,* vol. 16, no. 2, 1984, 44, note 9.

15   Gudkov and Levinson asked a question about a global "Zionist" conspiracy too. Within sampling error, their finding for the proportion of Russians who agree that a "Zionist" plot exists is nearly the same as my finding for Moscow. I am grateful to the authors for supplying some of their unpublished data to Andrei Degtyarev.

16   Together these variables account for only 6 per cent of the variation in antisemitic belief. R-square is sensitive to the distribution of cases across categories of the independent variables. If few cases fall into some categories of the independent variables, then the upper limit of R-square decreases. In the present case, this occurs with income and nationality. The low R-square does not therefore necessarily weaken my argument.

17   Rhonda L. Lenton, "Home versus career: Attitudes towards women's work among Russian women and men, 1992", *Canadian Journal of Sociology,* vol. 18, no. 3, 1993, 325-31.

18   As Sonja Margolina recently put it, "[t]he equation of 'Jews' and the 'West' in the sense of agents of modernization remains until today one of the great ideological clichés of premodern consciousness in the East.", Sonja Margolina, *Das Ende der Lügen: Rußand und die Juden im 20. Jahrhundert* (Berlin: Siedler Verlag, 1992), 8. For a similar conclusion regarding Slovakia see Zora Bútorová and Martin Bútora, "Wariness towards Jews as an expression of post-Communist panic: The case of Slovakia," *Czechoslovak Sociological Review,* Special Issue, no. 28, 1992, 92-106.

19   A few respondents gave other responses which I do not consider here. On the Russian far right see, for example, *Nationalities Papers,* Special Issue on *Pamyat,* vol. 19, no. 2, 1991.

20   *Antisemitism World Report 1993* (London: Institute of Jewish Affairs, 1993), 100-102, 104.

21   I tried to create a uni-dimensional scale measuring the intensity of Jewish perceptions of antisemitism but failed. No matter what combination of questionnaire items I used in the scale I could not achieve a Cronbach's-alpha reliability coefficient greater than .465. This strongly suggests that perceptions of antisemitism are not uni-dimensional.

22   *Antisemitism World Report 1992* (London: Institute of Jewish Affairs, 1992), 68. See, however, *Antisemitism World Report 1993,* 104.

23   *Antisemitism World Report 1992,* 68.

24   For a more technical justification for examining a single dimension see note 21.

25   In general, however, the income of Jews is above average. For example, the average income in Moscow in February-March 1993 was 11,625 roubles per month, *Sotsialno-ekonomicheskoe polozhenie rossiyskoy federatsii v yanvare-marte 1993 goda,* Ekonomichesky obzor no. 4, Goskomstat Rossii (Moscow: Respublikansky informatsionno-izdatelsky tsentr, 1993), 145. All the Moscow Jews in my survey were interviewed in those two months. Their

3 Russian immigrants present their papers on arrival at Israeli consulate, Moscow.

4 Kiev airport, departure.

average monthly income was 27,218 roubles, more than two and a third times above the city average. This difference appears *not* to be the result of Jews being more involved in the private sector than non-Jews (Mordechai Altshuler, "Jews and Russians—1991", *Yehudei brit ha-moatsot* (The Jews of the Soviet Union), vol. 15, 1992, 33). Thus 28 per cent of non-Jewish respondents in the October 1992 survey I conducted with Andrei Degtyarev worked at least partly in the private sector, compared to 29 per cent of Moscow Jews in the February-April 1993 survey I conducted with Rozalina Ryvkina. The income difference between the two groups appears to be mainly due to the different occupational structure, higher educational attainment and seniority of Jews. Note also that the *median* income for Moscow Jews was only 13,800 roubles per month. This implies that there are relatively few extremely wealthy Jews who pull up the mean. Although the median income for the general population is unknown, the difference between Jewish and population medians is undoubtedly far less than the difference between the means.

26 In the general population, however, it is the young who are most vulnerable to unemployment. For details on the social composition of the unemployed see Sheila Marnie, "How prepared is Russia for mass unemployment?", Radio Free Europe/Radio Liberty Special Report, 11 November 1992. On the special case of scientists see the results of a poll conducted among 300 Moscow scientists during the summer of 1991 as reported in Nikolai Popov, Roussina Volkova and Vadim Sazonov, "Unemployment in Science: Executive Summary" (Moscow: VTsIOM, 1991).

27 In Table 4.11 I collapsed a more detailed occupational breakdown.

28 I suspect that there is a reciprocal relationship between Jewishness and fear of antisemitism but I have not explored that possibility here so as to avoid technical complications.

29 V. O. Rukavishnikov *et al.*, "Social tension: Diagnosis and prognosis", *Sociological Research,* vol. 32, no. 2, 1993, 58.

30 Arthur Hertzberg, "Is anti-semitism dying out?", *The New York Review of Books,* 24 June 1993.

5 Emigration

THE SIZE AND DIRECTION OF THE EMIGRATION MOVEMENT, 1966-93

Sometime in mid-1993 the millionth Jew emigrated from the former USSR in the twenty-five years since 1968. During that period fewer than two-thirds of the emigrants settled in Israel. Over one-third settled elsewhere, mostly in the USA.

Those are rounded figures. Beneath their smooth contours lies more than a quarter-century of high political and human drama which has been recounted in precise detail by a host of participants and analysts. My intention here is not to provide yet another narrative account of the emigration movement. Rather, I will focus on just two themes. First, I will show that the development and demise of Soviet society, and the actions of the main parties involved in the emigration drama, caused enormous variation from year to year in both the number of Jews who left and in their choice of destinations.[1] Second, I will analyze data from my survey of Jews in Moscow, Kiev and Minsk, as well as from other sources, in order to hazard a prognosis of the future of the emigration movement.

Figure 5.1 tells the first part of the story in graphic form. It shows the number of emigrants who went to Israel and the number who went to the West each year from 1971 to 1993.[2] Table 5.1 helps make sense of the graph by dividing the history of the emigration movement into seven periods. Each period is characterized along three dimensions—the annual number of emigrants, the trend in the annual number of emigrants, and the annual proportion of emigrants who went to the West.

The emigration movement emerged out of a confluence of circumstances, the most fundamental of which I discussed in Chapter 2. Because of the social location they occupied, and the nature of Soviet nationality policy, the Jews had become redundant to the labour requirements of the Soviet federal state. From a broad point of view this was merely a variation on an old historical theme. The Jews migrated in large numbers to Eastern Europe when, beginning in the fifteenth century, the mercantile functions

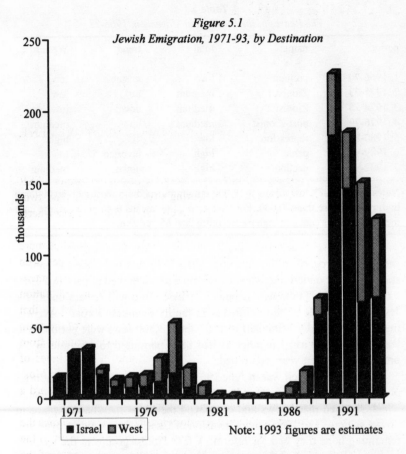

Figure 5.1
Jewish Emigration, 1971-93, by Destination

■ Israel ▩ West

Note: 1993 figures are estimates

they performed in the feudal economies of Western Europe became redundant. And they migrated in even larger numbers from Eastern Europe to North America under analogous circumstances four hundred years later. In a sense, major Jewish migrations have always heralded world-historical change. This was no less the case from the mid-1960s onwards than it was one or five centuries earlier.

The first phase of the emigration movement may be dated from the mid-1960s, when it had already become more difficult for some Jews to gain admission to the better institutions of higher education, find good jobs and obtain promotions. As one Soviet commentator noted only a few years later, "[t]he tasks confronting the system of people's education have been fulfilled and overfulfilled. . . . The national economy is close to

Table 5.1
The Phases of the Emigration Movement, 1966-93

period	name	total	trend	Western
1. 1966-70	prelude	low	unstable	low
2. 1971-73	Zionist 1	medium	up	low
3. 1974-75	Zionist 2	medium	down	low
4. 1976-79	post-Zionist	medium	up	medium
5. 1980-88	repression	low	"U"	high
6. 1989-91	panic	high	inverted "U"	low
7. 1992-93	decline	high	down	medium

Notes: For "total", low means 0-10,000 emigrants, medium means 11-70,000 and high means more than 70,000. For "Western", low means 0-40 per cent, medium means 41-65 per cent and high means more than 65 per cent.

saturation in regard to diploma specialists."[3] In this light one can understand the logic underlying Alexei Kosygin's much quoted remark in a 1966 Paris interview: "[T]he way is open", he said, "and will remain open" for Jews in the USSR to be reunified with family members abroad.[4] Accordingly, in 1966 and the first half of 1967 about 3,500 Jews were permitted to leave—about the same number as had been permitted to emigrate in the preceding eighteen years combined.[5]

The Arab-Israeli war in June 1967 brought an abrupt end to that brief policy change. It was replaced by a state-initiated "anti-Zionist" campaign which shocked many Jews and convinced them that they had no place in Soviet society. The 1968 Soviet invasion of Czechoslovakia destroyed any remaining hope they had for reform. A few Zionist groups in the recently annexed territories had functioned secretly since World War II and some new Zionist circles had been inspired by Israel's victory in the 1967 war. They now began to press urgently for the right to emigrate. That gave the regime added incentive to let Jews leave: emigration could serve as a safety valve for the release of Zionist dissidents. In 1970 the "Regulations on Entry into the USSR and Exit from the USSR" were revised to add fees and charges to the emigration process in anticipation of a substantially increased outflow, which began in earnest the following year. Nearly 13,000 Jews were permitted to emigrate from the USSR in 1971 on the pretext that they were being permitted to join family members abroad. That was over 25 per cent more than during the entire period 1948-70.

The second phase of the emigration movement stretched from 1971 to 1973. It was characterized by steadily increasing numbers of emigrants, the virtually unanimous selection of Israel as a destination and what from a later vantage point can be recognized as moderate annual emigration rates—roughly, between 13,000 and 35,000 emigrants per year. The movement's third stage differed in only one respect: between 1974 and 1975 the annual emigration rate declined to about 13,000.

This was the first of three cycles in the rate of emigration, each of increasing amplitude. The annual rate of emigration first peaked in 1973 and bottomed out in 1975, then crested again at a higher rate in 1979 and dropped to an even deeper trough by 1986, then reached its highest-ever point in 1990 and began to fall thereafter and until the time of this writing (August 1993).

It is tempting to view these fluctuations as a reflection of the cordiality of ties between the USA and the USSR/CIS.[6] Some analysts have thus argued that the first peak in emigration was preceded by a general warming of relations in the early 1970s—the period of *détente*. During that era the USA offered the USSR trade credits and Most Favoured Nation status in exchange for more Jewish emigration. Presumably, the first trough in the emigration rate was precipitated by Soviet anger over the collapse of trade talks between the two countries.

By the same reasoning, the peak of the second cycle was preceded by the Soviet Union giving way to US pressure, signing the Helsinki Final Act in 1975 and thereby pledging to make travel and emigration easier for its citizens. In contrast, the rapid fall in the rate of emigration after 1979 was due to the chilling of US-Soviet relations in the wake of the Soviet invasion of Afghanistan and the imposition of martial law in Poland.

Finally, the enormous surge in the emigration rate after 1988 was supposedly a reflection of *perestroyka*, the collapse of Communism and the new friendship that emerged between the USA and the CIS.

While superficially appealing, this "barometer thesis" is flawed, both logically and empirically. Specifically:

▪ It ignores the fact that the emigration movement began around 1966, several years before the *détente* era and the improvement of relations between the superpowers.

▪ It incorrectly assumes that the USA was able to exert substantial influence over Soviet domestic policy. The plain fact is, however, that in no year did Soviet-US commerce ever amount to more than 10 per cent of Soviet trade with the West. Also, whenever the USA tried to use trade sanctions to control Soviet behaviour the Soviets simply turned to Germany, Japan or Canada for Western goods.[7] If anything, what the collapse of trade negotiations in 1974 demonstrates is that the USA *lacked* leverage with the USSR. Negotiations broke down because the USA was demanding what the Soviets saw as too many human rights concessions in exchange for more trade. More generally, the breakdown confirms that the Soviet Union "never, not even in the times of its greatest weakness, permitted concessions in its internal regime to become the object of diplomatic negotiations."[8]

▪ Although the emigration rate started to rise again in 1976, Soviet-American relations were deteriorating on many fronts. This was the period when Soviet and Cuban forces invaded Angola, when the USSR intervened militarily in the Horn of Africa and when protracted SALT negotiations seemed to be getting nowhere.

▪ Only by some perverse logic would the USSR have decided to cut emigration in response to American condemnation of the 1979 invasion of Afghanistan, the imposition of trade sanctions and the boycott of the 1980 Moscow Olympics. Would it not have made elementary good sense to allow more Jews out in order to curry favour with the USA and mitigate American fury?

▪ Some commentators argue that the volume of US-Soviet trade is a good indicator of the warmth of relations between the two countries. If so, it is revealing that between 1971 and 1987 there was no statistically significant relationship between the annual volume of US-Soviet trade and the annual rate of Soviet Jewish emigration.[9]

▪ The rise in the emigration rate after 1988 was undeniably connected to *perestroyka* and the collapse of Communism. Whether the growing friendship between the USSR/ CIS and the USA had any bearing on the course of the third emigration cycle is, however, far from clear. After all, the emigration rate began to fall rapidly again after 1990, but US-CIS relations remained cordial.

On the basis of these considerations I conclude that the warmth of USSR/CIS-US ties has not been the principal influence on the rate of emigration, although it has undoubtedly had some influence. Rather, emigration rates seem to respond most sensitively to two internal factors— (1) ongoing debates at the highest levels of the USSR/ CIS leadership about labour-force requirements, which have fluctuated from one decade to the next; and (2) emigrants' perceptions of, and preferences among, emigration opportunities, which have fluctuated in accordance with the social composition of the emigrants and the immigration policies of Western states.

The importance of emigrants' perceptions and preferences can be seen most vividly if we reconsider the post-1973 slump in the emigration rate. Interestingly, by dividing the emigration wave into two components—emigrants headed to Israel and those headed elsewhere—we see that there was a steady *increase* in the number of emigrants headed elsewhere from 1974 to 1980 and a more or less steady increase in the *proportion* of Western-bound emigrants straight through to 1988 (see Figure 5.1). The mid-1970s slump was actually a decline only in the number of Israel-bound emigrants.

After 1973 fewer emigrants chose to go to Israel partly because the initial pool of Zionist and religious activists had already left the USSR. Later emigrants tended to be more assimilated and less interested in living in the Jewish state. That was partly reflected in the regional origins of the emigrants. From 1966 to 1973 the great majority of Soviet Jewish emigrants came from peripheral regions where Jews were less assimilated, such as the Baltic republics, Moldova, Georgia, western Ukraine and Belarus. After 1973 the proportion of emigrants from Russia, eastern Ukraine and Belarus, where Jews were more assimilated, grew steadily. Surveys conducted at the time revealed a corresponding shift in emigrants' motives for leaving. While many pre-1974 emigrants tended to say that they were leaving due to ethnic discrimination and the desire to live in the Jewish state, post-1973 emigrants tended to express more universalistic and pragmatic motives such as wanting to live in a democracy or in a country where they could enjoy freedom of cultural expression and a higher standard of living. Also important in causing the shift away from Israel as a destination was the 1973 Arab-Israeli war, which underlined the dangers of living in the Middle East. Finally, it soon became apparent that countries other than Israel, especially the USA, were prepared to accept immigrants from the Soviet Union. As this knowledge spread, and as Soviet Jews established a foothold in countries other than Israel, the rate and proportion of Soviet Jewish emigrants bound for countries other than Israel rose.[10]

In 1980 the emigration rate again began to plummet. This was, I believe, due mainly to perceptions of changing Soviet labour-force requirements by a leadership intent on rescuing the Soviet system from itself.[11] Growing problems with the command economy had been evident since the late 1950s and feeble attempts at reform had been made on several occasions, most notably during the Khrushchev era. In the early 1980s, however, the leadership made a last-ditch effort to prevent further declines in productivity and the standard of living—but all within the rigid framework of the Communist system. *Within the limits of the Communist system*, one of the more serious problems they faced was a large and growing labour deficit. This had direct implications for emigration policy.

Arkady Shevchenko spent twenty years in the Soviet Foreign Ministry before defecting to the USA. He is therefore well qualified to speak on the question of emigration policy. In his 1985 memoirs Shevchenko noted that in the Soviet leadership

[a]t any given moment those who protest the loss of skilled technical manpower may have an edge over those who think it possible to obtain Western concessions by clearing the country of a resented minority. At another time the majority view can change. All that is certain is that the issue is a troublesome one that can generate different responses whenever it is raised.[12]

In the early 1980s hardline Communists who feared the loss of technical manpower won out. Labour shortages had become especially acute in the European part of the USSR, where the overwhelming majority of Jews resided. Experts estimated that between 1985 and 1990 the size of the working-age population in the non-Muslim areas of the USSR would actually decline.[13] From the point of view of the Communist leadership, the emigration of substantial numbers of highly trained Jews from precisely those areas threatened with the greatest labour shortages hardly seemed like a good idea under the circumstances. The "back-lash accusing the leadership of provoking a deplorable drain of scientific, cultural, academic and moral capital" predicted by Peter Reddaway was at hand.[14]

This background allows us to make sense of a Central Committee letter on the "Jewish question" that was read at closed Party meetings in 1979. The circular, reported in a *samizdat* journal, emphasized the need to make admission to jobs and higher education somewhat *easier* for Jews while, at the same time, stepping up "anti-Zionist" propaganda and making emigration more difficult.[15] The anti-emigration campaign continued until the advent of Gorbachev. As Theodore Friedgut remarked:

Brezhnev's focus on domestic economic problems was inherited by Andropov, who turned it into a campaign of discipline, eradication of corruption and restoration of a work ethic. The anti-emigration atmosphere was needed for this campaign too. The Jews had to be shown that emigration was out of the question, at least for the coming years, and that in their own interests, as well as those of the Soviet economy, they should live normal Soviet lives.[16]

Some concern over labour shortages extended into the *perestroyka* era. Thus in 1987 a "very senior Soviet official" told the Vice-President of the Canadian Jewish Congress that the advocates of *perestroyka* placed a premium on the technical and managerial jobs for which Jews were especially well trained, as a result of which the authorities were increasingly reluctant to let many more Jews leave.[17] By the late 1980s, however, that had become the minority view.

Most analysts came around to the opinion that serious labour dislocations would result from dismantling the central planning apparatus, rolling back price subsidies, scaling down the bloated state bureaucracy, ending Central Bank subsidies to inefficient industries and passing bankruptcy laws. For example, in 1988 Vladimir Kostakov, Director of the Economics Research Institute, GOSPLAN SSSR, projected that between 1986 and 2000 labour productivity would increase 15 to 25 per cent faster than national income. This meant that 13 to 19 million fewer Soviet workers would be needed in material production by the end of the century. Meanwhile, in *Pravda* it was estimated that administrative and managerial cadres would shrink by 50 per cent or more, leaving an additional 9 million people out of work. Kostakov expected that surplus labour would be absorbed by increasing the size of the pensioned population, offering more generous maternity leave, encouraging full-time rather than part-time education, shortening the working week and expanding the service sector. But even before the collapse of Communism in 1991, most Russian commentators recognized that, at least in the short-to-medium-term, widespread unemployment was a much more likely scenario than the growth of a Swedish-style welfare state.[18]

The panic emigration following 1988 ought to be viewed in the clear light of these structural circumstances. In the period 1989-91 many CIS Jews feared that antisemitic pogroms would break out. Economic ruin and political instability, including ethnic warfare and a coup attempt, acted as additional incentives to leave. The final years of the Communist regime and the disintegration of the USSR witnessed a general liberalization of which emigration policy was one part. Certainly all of these factors contributed heavily to the unprecedented flow of emigrants from the USSR/ CIS. Nevertheless, what made the massive emigration possible in the first place was that the leaders of a society moving away from central planning foresaw the danger of massive labour surpluses. They apparently regarded emigration as one means of easing the burden.

Israel was eager to welcome all new arrivals. Ironically, the USA and other Western countries were not. Much had changed in twenty years. The West had promoted freedom of movement when the world economy was vibrant and the influx of immigrants from the Soviet Union was relatively modest and stretched over a couple of decades. But in the midst of a deep recession and tight budgets the task of absorbing a million or more Jews from the USSR—and, potentially, many more non-Jews—was simply out of the question.[19] In October 1989 the USA imposed new regulations denying Soviet Jews automatic refugee status and thereby restricting their influx. Thereafter it became apparent that the USA was prepared to allow only about 40,000 Soviet Jews to enter annually.[20] As a result, the proportion of emigrants "choosing" to go to Israel shot up once again. In September 1989 97 per cent of Soviet Jewish emigrants chose *not* to go to Israel. Once the American restrictions were imposed that proportion fell to about 20 per cent and remained at that level until 1991.

The year 1992 marked the beginning of the last phase of the emigration movement listed in Table 5.1. While the number of emigrants going to countries other than Israel more than doubled over the 1991 figure, the number going to Israel fell by more than half. As a result, the proportion of emigrants choosing not to go to Israel rose above the 50 per cent level again and the total rate of emigration dropped substantially; the projected 1993 total was just over a third of the 1991 total. The panic was subsiding.

Several circumstances changed the mood of CIS Jewry, causing drops in the emigration rate and the proportion choosing to go to Israel. The predicted pogroms did not occur. The August 1991 *putsch* was a failure. For some Jews in the region the collapse of the Communist system held out the promise, however faint, of a better life. Meanwhile, for all its efforts, Israel found it extremely difficult to absorb the third of a million new immigrants who arrived on its shores in just two years—a feat proportionate to expecting the USA to house and find jobs for about 16 million arrivals in the same period or Germany to cope with over 6 million immigrants. Letters from Israel to friends and relatives in the USSR/CIS were very discouraging.[21]

Indeed, what is surprising is that the 1992 emigration figure broke the 100,000 mark at all. It did so partly due to a quite unexpected development. Suddenly, quietly and defying all apparent logic, Germany increased its intake of CIS Jews to over 2,000 a month.[22] Here was a country facing a flat economy and the mammoth task of modernizing former East Germany. Its open-door immigration policy burdened it with absorbing hundreds of thousands of ethnic Germans from Russia and other asylum-seekers from Eastern Europe annually. Germany had, moreover, to manage increasingly violent anti-immigration sentiment together with an angry backlash on the part of Turkish *Gastarbeiter* and sympathetic native Germans. In this context it is difficult to understand why CIS Jews should have suddenly been so welcome. The only possible explanation is that they served a useful ideological function, allowing the German government to assuage war guilt and demonstrate the absence of racism in its ranks.[23] In any case, in 1993 Germany passed restrictive asylum laws, its economy remained stagnant and the mood of sections of its population remained ugly. It is therefore doubtful that the immigration of CIS Jews will continue for much longer at the 1992 level.

In view of these recent developments—declining emigration rates since 1990, serious absorption problems in Israel, restricted immigration opportunities in the USA, a likely downturn in immigration opportunities in Germany—it seems worthwhile asking what will become of the emigration movement in the near future. How many Jews still want to leave the CIS? Why? What are the social determinants of their decisions to stay or leave and, in the latter case, to choose one country over another? We may now return to the survey of Jews in Moscow, Kiev and Minsk in order to shed light on those questions.

HOW MANY WANT TO LEAVE?

Under certain circumstances virtually every Jew in the former USSR would emigrate. One can speculate what those conditions might involve—complete economic and political anarchy combined with widespread antisemitic violence at home, wide-open immigration regulations combined with abundant job opportunities in the West and Israel. In reality, however, none of those conditions exists. For all the troubles suffered by Russia, Ukraine and Belarus—hyperinflation, declining production, rising crime rates, environmental degradation, intense political conflict between reformers and conservatives, comparatively high levels of anti-Jewish feeling—most Jews in my sample intend to stay put. Specifically, when asked whether they plan to emigrate, 57 per cent of the respondents answered "no", 14 per cent said "don't know" and 29 per cent replied "yes". Fourteen per cent of the respondents said they planned to emigrate to the USA. Only

8 per cent said they planned to emigrate to Israel. Seven per cent expressed
the intention to leave for other countries and 2 per cent had not decided
where they would go (see Table 5.2, columns one and two).

Table 5.2
Emigration Plans of Respondents and Jewish Population of Former USSR

	respondents		former USSR (est.)	
	frequency	per cent	frequency (in '000s)	per cent
not planning to emigrate	572	57	538	47
don't know	141	14	160	14
planning to emigrate to				
Israel	78	8	183	16
USA	136	14		
Canada	23	2		
Australia	17	2	263	23
Germany	13	1		
other	3	0		
don't know	18	2		
total	1,001	100	1,144	100

Note: Column 1 adds up to 1,001 due to weighting.

Unfortunately, one cannot mechanically manipulate these figures to
arrive at a precise estimate of the Jewish emigration potential of the entire
territory of the former USSR. Strictly speaking, my survey data entitle me
to generalize only about the Jews of Moscow, Kiev and Minsk, who comprise 28 per cent of the Jews in Russia, Ukraine and Belarus. Roughly
speaking, however, it is difficult to imagine that figures for the rest of
Russia and the other large cities of Ukraine (Kharkov and Odessa) would
differ much from those in the first two columns of Table 5.2; the socio-
demographic profile of Jews in these other areas is quite similar to the
profile of Jews in the three cities where my sample was drawn.[24] I estimate,
therefore, that the findings in the first two columns of Table 5.2 hold approximately for 55 per cent of Jews in the former USSR.[25]
    As far as the remaining 45 per cent of the Jewish population are
concerned, one can state with certainty that their emigration potential is
higher than that reflected in the first two columns of Table 5.2 and that a

larger proportion of them wish to emigrate to Israel. As we will see below, strength of Jewish identity varies proportionately with emigration potential and with propensity to choose Israel as a destination; and there are proportionately more Jewish Jews living outside Russia and the large cities of Ukraine. The proportions involved are, however, unknown. My guess—and I state emphatically that this is only a guess—is that the emigration potential of the rest of the CIS is similar in proportionate terms to that of Minsk alone (for which see Table 5.6, panel 1). I thus assume that 35 per cent of these other Jews are not planning to emigrate, 15 per cent of them do not know whether they will emigrate, 25 per cent of them intend to move to Israel and 25 per cent intend to move to countries other than Israel or are not sure where they will go.

Combining my approximate estimate for 55 per cent of the population with my much more speculative estimate for the remaining 45 per cent, I arrive at the conclusion that, in the first quarter of 1993, about 47 per cent of the Jews in the former USSR (538,000 people) were *not* planning to emigrate (see Table 5.2, columns three and four). Fourteen per cent (160,000 people) were unsure, 16 per cent planned to go to Israel (183,000 people) and 23 per cent (263,000 people) planned to go to other countries or did not know where they would end up.

Although all these figures are based partly on educated guesswork, one's confidence in them increases when they are placed alongside the results of two independent estimates. The first comes from a newspaper poll conducted in Moscow by Professor Ryvkina in December 1991.[26] Ryvkina had a questionnaire printed in *Yevreyskaya gazeta*, a Jewish newspaper with a circulation of 25,000-30,000 published in Moscow. Ninety-three self-selected experts in Jewish affairs completed questionnaires. They estimated that 61 per cent of Jews would emigrate from the USSR. That is 8 per cent above my estimate of the number of people in the former USSR who are planning to emigrate plus those who are still unsure whether they will emigrate. The 1991 poll was based on a small sample and was conducted during the panic emigration of the very early 1990s, when expectations concerning the number of Jews likely to leave the region were temporarily inflated. Nonetheless, the results of the poll are in line with the results of my survey.

Second, in my survey, respondents were themselves asked to estimate how many Jews would emigrate from the former USSR. The respondents were not experts in Jewish affairs but they tended to be highly educated and had the great virtue of being able to assess the situation "on the ground", as it were. Of the 86 per cent who ventured an opinion, 11 per cent said that "nearly all" CIS Jews would emigrate, 58 per cent answered "a majority", 24 per cent said "half" and 7 per cent replied "a minority". If "nearly all" means 90 per cent, "a majority" means 60 per cent, "half" means 50 per cent and "a minority" means 20 per cent, then the average estimate of my respondents is 58 per cent—5 per cent above my estimate for the number of people in the former USSR who are planning to emigrate plus those who are still unsure whether they will emigrate. I conclude that both independent estimates are in line with my own. Statistically speaking, one can be 95 per cent confident that the difference between my estimate, on the one hand, and both Professor Ryvkina's and my respondents', on the other, is due to chance.[27]

Of course, all estimates can easily be turned upside down by unforeseen developments, as students of Soviet and CIS society know better than most. Moreover, there is a difference between planning to go to a particular country and actually arriving there; United States immigration quotas may, for example, force some emigrants who would otherwise wind up in the USA to go to Israel.[28] Much depends also on what the "don't knows" eventually decide to do. That said, the best information available suggests that Natan Sharansky, among many others, was wrong when he wrote in 1992 that "millions [of Jews] are on their way" out of the former USSR.[29] So was Israeli President Ezer Weizmann, who claimed on Israeli television on 29 June 1993 (Channel 1) that 2 million Jews in the CIS were ready to emigrate. There are no millions. If conditions remain what they are today, and even in the unlikely event that all the "don't knows" elect to emigrate, it seems that as of 1993 about 606,000 more Jews plan on leaving the former Soviet Union. In the equally unlikely event that all the "don't knows" elect to go to Israel, that country can expect at most about 345,000 more Jews to arrive from the former USSR, a figure well below most current Israeli projections, which still speak of close to a million new arrivals between 1993 and 2000.[30] (Another set of estimates of immigration to Israel and elsewhere, based on a projection of current trends, is offered in the concluding section of this chapter.)

WHY DO THEY WANT TO GO?

The foregoing analysis raises a number of subsidiary issues. Why do so many Jews plan to leave the CIS? What keeps so many Jews there? Why do so few plan to go to Israel? Respondents were asked questions about all these issues. Their answers reveal some interesting patterns.

Table 5.3
Reasons for Wanting to Emigrate (first three choices)

	frequency	per cent
q77-for the sake of children's future	176	24
q75-to improve standard of living	129	18
q80-no expected improvement in situation	128	17
economic subtotal	433	59
q76-political instability	103	14
q78-fear of antisemitism and pogroms	99	13
q79-fear of violence	41	6
ethnic-political subtotal	243	33
q81-to keep family together	59	8
total	735	100

The 429 respondents who said they were planning to emigrate were asked to review a list of seven options and select their three chief motives for wanting to leave. Their responses are not quite as enlightening as they could have been because, due to oversight, the list did not include options indicating cultural or ethnic affinity with the West and with Israel (which I strongly expect would have been infrequently selected in any case). Basically, Table 5.3 shows that Jews are motivated to leave more for economic reasons (59 per cent of responses) than for reasons of antisemitic persecution, general fear of violence and political instability (33 per cent) or family reunification (8 per cent). One certainly can-not conclude on this basis that, in general, Jewish emigrants from the CIS are refugees. The data do suggest, however, that a large minority of them could be so defined without any stretching of the Western legal definition.

Respondents were also asked what ties them to their country. They were allowed to choose up to three options from a fixed list of nine. Table 5.4 details their responses. It reveals a pattern nearly the reverse of Table 5.3. One may infer that economic ties keep only a small minority of respondents rooted in their country while familial and especially cultural ties, broadly defined, loom large. Thus while only 12 per cent of responses

Table 5.4
Ties to One's Country (first three choices)

	frequency	per cent
q100-accustomed to it	715	29
q106-closely connected to culture	438	18
cultural subtotal	1153	47
q103-unwilling to leave relatives	375	15
q104-unwilling to leave friends	303	12
familial subtotal	678	27
q99-have a good job here	114	5
q102-hope to increase standard of living here	100	4
q101-hope to establish business here	67	3
economic subtotal	281	12
q107-old age, weak health	195	8
q105-hope for political stability here	157	6
total	2464	100

indicate the importance of economic ties, 27 per cent suggest that family ties prevent Jews from emigrating and 47 per cent of responses suggest that cultural affinity is the most important factor keeping them where they are.

Finally, let us consider why respondents planning to leave for the West do not select Israel as their destination. Up to three choices were permitted from a fixed list of seven options.[31] As Table 5.5 shows, cultural reasons were the most frequently chosen (31 per cent of responses). That is, people planning to leave the CIS often choose to go to countries other than Israel because they would find it too difficult to live in an atmosphere of Jewish culture or to learn Hebrew. Economic reasons for choosing a country other than Israel follow closely in importance (29 per cent). Indeed, the lack of good jobs in Israel is the single most frequent justification for deciding to go to other destinations. Thus when respondents who chose other destinations were asked whether they would go to Israel if they could

Table 5.5
Reasons for Not Wanting to Emigrate to Israel (first three choices)

	frequency	per cent
q85-difficulty of living in Jewish culture	90	18
q88-Hebrew too difficult to learn	68	13
cultural subtotal	190	31
q83-not enough good jobs there	143	28
q84-fear of losing business here	5	1
economic subtotal	148	29
q87-few friends and/ or relatives in Israel	96	19
q86-Arab-Israeli conflict and war threat	71	14
q90-too old or weak	34	7
total	507	100

secure a job comparable to the one they currently hold, fully 31 per cent per cent said "yes" (78,000 people in population terms). Other reasons for choosing a destination other than Israel include having too few friends and/ or relatives in Israel (19 per cent of responses), the Arab-Israeli conflict and the threat of war (14 per cent), and being too old or weak to live in Israel (7 per cent).

I conclude that while Jews who are planning to emigrate are motivated mainly by economic factors, Jews who do not want to emigrate are motivated principally by cultural affinity for their homeland. Meanwhile, among those planning to leave for the West, a combination of economic and cultural factors dissuade them from choosing Israel as a destination. These findings should interest Jewish policy-makers outside the CIS. Cultural predispositions are more difficult to change than economic opportunities and altering each would have different effects. Specifically, investing to create more good jobs in Israel would have a marked impact on shifting the flow of CIS emigrants from the West to Israel but would not substantially increase the number of Jews leaving the CIS. Increasing the number of departures would require, above all else, a long-term campaign aimed at a cultural reorientation to which most CIS Jews do not appear amenable (see Chapter 3).

DETERMINANTS OF MIGRATION PLANS

Now that we have a sense of approximately how many Jews wish to leave the CIS, where they wish to settle, and why they wish to leave, we can examine the social factors underlying their emigration plans. In order to simplify my presentation I combined two questions concerning emigration plans—"Do you intend to emigrate from the country?" and "To which country are you planning to immigrate?"—into a single indicator. In the combined version of these questions there were four possible response categories: (1) No, I do not plan to emigrate; (2) I do not know whether I will emigrate; (3) I plan on emigrating to the West; (4) I plan on emigrating to Israel. Table 5.6 sets out the list of factors that are statistically significantly associated with migration plans at the .05 probability level. Let us quickly sift through the numbers.[32]

The proportion of Jews planning to emigrate increases as one moves from Moscow to Kiev to Minsk; from older to younger age categories; from married and widowed people to never-married, separated and divorced individuals; from people with no children living abroad to people with one, two or more children living outside the country; from retired to employed individuals to homemakers to unemployed people to students; and from people who have no friends or relatives abroad to those who do. It is thus evident that the weaker one's social attachments to one's country— as determined by youth, lack of marital ties, and lack of employment ties— and the stronger one's social attachments abroad—as measured by number of family and friendship ties outside the country—the greater the propensity to leave.

The picture is more complicated when one shifts attention to the proportion of Jews planning to emigrate to Israel. The relationships listed above hold for some variables (city, number of children abroad, having friends and relatives in Israel and, somewhat suprisingly, having friends in the USA) but they are considerably weaker or non-existent for other variables. Consider age. While 61 per cent of the respondents between the ages of 18 and 29 said they plan on emigrating, that figure falls to 22 per cent for respondents 60 years of age and older. Clearly, emigration is mainly for the young. Meanwhile, 10 per cent of the respondents between the ages of 18 and 29 plan to emigrate to Israel, little different from the 8 per cent of people 60 years and older who expressed the same intention. Israel is nearly as likely to attract older immigrants as younger ones. A similar story can be told for marital status, work status, having friends and relatives in countries other than Israel and having relatives in the USA:

Table 5.6
Correlates of Emigration Plans (in per cent; n in parentheses)

		emigration plans			
	no	don't know	West	Israel	total
q5-city					
Moscow	63	15	16	6	100 (535)
Kiev	56	12	23	9	100 (329)
Minsk	41	17	25	18	101 (119)
chi-square = 37.19, d.f. = 6, p = .000; tau-c = 0.127					
q8-age					
18-29	39	22	29	10	100 (177)
30-39	52	19	23	6	100 (151)
40-49	59	16	18	8	101 (210)
50-59	62	12	19	8	101 (279)
60-90	78	6	9	8	101 (166)
chi-square = 65.23, d.f. = 12, p = .000; tau-c = -0.160					
q10-marital status					
never married	48	22	23	8	101 (143)
married	60	14	20	7	101 (680)
separated/ div.	49	12	22	17	100 (94)
widowed	75	10	5	10	100 (66)
chi-square = 34.29, d.f. = 9, p = .000; tau-c = -0.027					
q13-number of children abroad					
0	60	15	19	7	101 (892)
1	44	13	26	19	102 (69)
2+	28	15	31	26	100 (11)
chi-square = 22.16, d.f. = 6, p = .001; tau-c = 0.053					
q14-work status					
retired	69	7	14	11	101 (196)
employed	58	17	18	7	100 (653)
homemaker	50	12	35	4	101 (38)
unemployed	44	4	41	12	101 (29)
student	36	28	30	6	100 (54)
chi-square = 50.99, d.f. = 12, p = .000; tau-c = 0.081					
q19-work satisfaction					
yes	61	15	16	7	99 (474)
no	51	14	27	9	101 (135)
chi-square = 8.44, d.f. = 3, p = .038; tau-c = 0.083					

Table 5.6 (cont'd)
Correlates of Emigration Plans (in per cent; n in parentheses)

		emigration plans			
	no	don't know	West	Israel	total
q21-sat. with work conditions					
satisfied	63	17	15	6	101 (427)
not satisfied	49	16	26	9	100 (188)
chi-square = 14.74, d.f. = 3, p = .000; tau-c = 0.133					
q22-sat. with managers at work					
satisfied	63	18	14	6	101 (497)
not satisfied	41	6	39	14	100 (88)
chi-square = 47.18, d.f. = 3, p = .000; tau-c = 0.150					
q23-sat. with colleagues at work					
satisfied	60	17	18	6	101 (593)
not satisfied	33	19	28	20	100 (25)
chi-square = 12.71, d.f. = 3, p = .005; tau-c = 0.051					
q24-sat. with post					
satisfied	60	17	16	6	99 (486)
not satisfied	54	10	27	9	100 (115)
chi-square = 10.74, d.f. = 3, p = .013; tau-c = 0.063					
q25-sat. with opportunities for advancement					
satisfied	62	18	15	5	100 (211)
not satisfied	55	14	21	10	100 (271)
chi-square = 8.39, d.f. = 3, p = .036; tau-c = 0.104					
q40-sat. with occupational position					
satisfied	68	13	14	5	100 (470)
not satisfied	46	17	27	10	100 (370)
chi-square = 43.46, d.f. = 3, p = .000; tau-c = 0.231					
q92-family or rels. in Israel					
yes	52	17	20	11	100 (584)
no	69	9	18	4	100 (363)
chi-square = 35.60, d.f. = 3, p=.000; tau-c = -0.166					
q93-family or rels. in US					
yes	50	15	27	9	101 (510)
no	68	13	11	8	100 (434)
chi-square = 42.16, d.f. = 3, p = .000; tau-c = -0.183					

Table 5.6 (cont'd)
Correlates of Emigration Plans (in per cent; n in parentheses)

	no	don't know	West	Israel	total
		emigration plans			

q94-family or rels. in other Western country

	no	don't know	West	Israel	total
yes	50	19	24	7	100 (205)
no	61	12	18	8	99 (714)

chi-square = 11.07, d.f. = 3, p = .011; tau-c = -0.062

q95-friends in Israel

yes	52	15	23	10	100 (633)
no	70	14	13	4	101 (337)

chi-square = 35.92, d.f. = 3, p = .000; tau-c = -0.185

q96-friends in US

yes	50	14	26	10	100 (560)
no	69	15	10	6	100 (408)

chi-square = 49.48, d.f. = 3, p = .000; tau-c = -0.208

q97-friends in other Western country

yes	51	17	26	7	101 (295)
no	62	13	17	9	101 (669)

chi-square = 16.82, d.f. = 3, p = .001; tau-c = -0.086

q108-feeling about Israel

hist. motherland	40	18	25	17	100 (197)
eminent state	57	14	18	11	100 (144)
like other states/ no att.	62	14	19	5	100 (511)

chi-square = 41.77, d.f. = 6, p = .000; tau-c = -0.150

q123-personally suffered antisemitism

yes	51	14	25	10	100 (539)
no	69	13	14	4	100 (326)

chi-square = 34.27, d.f. = 3, p = .000; tau-c = -0.196

q162-political system if 1-2 years

freer	60	18	15	7	100 (142)
same	58	14	17	11	100 (334)
less free	50	11	32	8	101 (236)

chi-square = 23.95, d.f. = 6, p = .001; tau-c = 0.079

Table 5.6 (cont'd)
Correlates of Emigration Plans (in per cent; n in parentheses)

	no	don't know	West	Israel	total
		emigration plans			
q163-confidence in own future					
yes	68	13	10	9	100 (161)
no	56	13	22	8	99 (684)
chi-square = 12.71, d.f. = 3, p = .005; tau-c = 0.077					
Jewishness scale					
low	75	13	11	2	101 (329)
medium	61	16	20	3	100 (327)
high	39	14	28	19	100 (326)
chi-square = 135.88, d.f. = 6, p =.000; tau-c = 0.283					

Note: Percentages do not necessarily add up to 100 due to rounding.

none of these factors exerts a discernible impact on one's tendency to emigrate to Israel.

Apart from the sociodemographic factors just discussed, Table 5.6 shows that three other sets of social forces affect respondents' migration plans. The first set relates to various facets of one's work environment. Note that it is job dissatisfaction as a professional issue, not as a pecuniary concern, that drives people to emigrate. Thus migration plans have nothing to do with actual income levels or levels of satisfaction with earnings. Respondents are, however, more inclined to plan to emigrate if they are dissatisfied with colleague and management relations at work, with actual working conditions, with their posts and with opportunities for advancement. In general, CIS Jews are extraordinarily dedicated to their jobs. The inability to achieve professional and intellectual fulfillment drives many of them out of the country. Note also that professional frustration also tends to increase respondents' propensity to choose Israel as a destination, although to a lesser degree than it affects the decision to leave in the first place.

A third set of factors influencing migration plans concerns Jewishness and the experience of antisemitism. It is the more Jewish Jews and those who have personally experienced antisemitism who are more inclined to plan to emigrate and to choose Israel as a destination.

Finally, being pessimistic about the prospects for democracy in one's country and lacking confidence in one's personal future are associated with planning to emigrate. These attitudes do not, however, increase the likelihood of choosing Israel as a destination.

Many of the variables in Table 5.6 tell us virtually the same thing. For example, age and marital status are similarly related to emigration plans and they are also related to each other (young people are more likely never to have been married and old people are more likely to be widows or widowers). Does age have an effect on emigration plans independent of the effect it shares with marital status? Which other variables have such independent effects and how strong are they? Table 5.7 presents a multiple regression analysis that answers these questions, eliminating redundancy and reducing the information in Table 5.6 to more vivid and informative proportions.

Table 5.7
Multiple Regression of Emigration Plans

question	slope (b)	standard error	standardized slope (beta)	t
sociodemographics				
q8-age	-.16	.02	-.21	7.29
q13-# child. abroad	.39	.09	.13	4.44
q96-friends USA	.21	.06	.10	3.65
q5-city size	.10	.04	.07	2.55
Jewish factors				
Jewishness scale	.04	.003	.33	11.08
q123-fear antisem.	.18	.06	.08	2.81
work factors				
q40-occ. satisfaction	-.21	.06	-.10	-3.31
q23-coll. relations	-.38	.18	-.06	-2.15

intercept = 1.92; n = 1,001; adjusted R^2 = .25

At least two variables from three of the four blocs isolated above exert a statistically significant and independent effect on emigration plans. The bloc of four sociodemographic variables—age, number of children living abroad, city of residence and friendship ties in the USA—exerts the greatest causal impact on emigration plans. Next is the bloc of two Jewish factors—Jewishness and fear of antisemitism. Indeed, the scale of Jewish identity and practice is by far the single most important determinant of emigration plans. The bloc of two work-related factors exerts less than 40 per cent of the causal weight of the Jewish factors. Listing each variable in order of importance, one's propensity to emigrate and to choose Israel as a destination is associated with relatively high levels of Jewish identity and practice, comparative youth, having more rather than fewer children abroad, having friends in the USA, being dissatisfied with one's work, fearing antisemitism, living in Minsk rather than Kiev and in Kiev rather than Moscow, and being dissatisfied with collegial relations at work.

EMIGRATION PROJECTIONS, 1994-99

In ending this chapter I want to engage in what may well prove to be a foolhardy exercise. I want to project the rate and destination of Jewish emigration from the CIS until the end of the century. The reader should be under no illusion about what these projections mean. *They are not predictions.* Rather, they merely extrapolate from current trends in the emigration movement and certain of my survey results, which are themselves based in part on educated guesswork. Specifically, Table 5.8 makes two assumptions: (1) The average annual decline in the rate of emigration was 18 per cent in the period 1990-93. I assume that this trend will continue to 1994. From 1994 to 1999 I assume that the emigration rate will drop at a rate of 10 per cent per year, reflecting the diminishing pool of potential emigrants. (2) About half the emigrants went to Israel in 1992 and 1993, but the survey-based estimates in Table 5.2 suggest that this figure will drop to one-third at the most. In Table 5.8 I assume that the proportion drops evenly to one-third by the end of the century.

Bearing in mind the important qualifications introduced above, Table 5.8 gives an extremely rough idea of how the emigration movement may develop until the end of the century. In brief, it suggests that the annual number of emigrants going to Israel may drop from about 51,000 in 1994 to about 20,000 in 1999, for a total of about 204,000 over the six-year span. The annual number of emigrants going to countries other than Israel may decline more gradually from about 51,000 in 1994 to about 41,000 in 1999, for a total of about 276,000. Table 5.8 also gives somewhat higher and less realistic maximum figures. My best guess, therefore, is that somewhere between 204,000 and 275,000 CIS emigrants will go to Israel between 1994 and 1999. Between 276,000 and 368,000 of them will go to other destinations. This will not spell the end of the Jewish community in the former USSR. It will, however, mark the end of one of its most important chapters.

Table 5.8
Projected CIS Emigration, 1994-99 (in '000s; per cent in parentheses)

	Israel	West	total
1994	51.3 (50.0)	51.3 (50.0)	102.5 (100.0)
1995	43.4 (47.0)	48.9 (53.0)	92.3 (100.0)
1996	35.7 (43.0)	47.3 (57.0)	83.3 (100.0)
1997	29.1 (39.0)	45.6 (61.0)	74.7 (100.0)
1998	24.9 (37.0)	42.4 (63.0)	67.3 (100.0)
1999	20.0 (33.0)	40.5 (67.0)	60.5 (100.0)
total	204.4 (42.5)	276.0 (57.4)	480.6 (99.9)
maximum	275.0	368.0	481.0

Note: The maxima are calculated from Table 5.2 minus 1993 emigration figures. The maximum total does not equal the sum of its components because each maximum is calculated independently on the assumption that it contains all the "don't knows". Some other totals do not equal the sum of their components due to rounding.

NOTES

1   In this section I draw on Robert J. Brym, "The changing rate of Jewish emigration from the USSR: Some lessons from the 1970s", *Soviet Jewish Affairs*, vol. 15, no. 2, 1985, 23-35; Robert J. Brym, "Soviet Jewish emigration: A statistical test of two theories", *Soviet Jewish Affairs*, vol. 18, no. 3, 1988, 15-23; Victor Zaslavsky and Robert J. Brym, *Soviet-Jewish Emigration and Soviet Nationality Policy* (London: Macmillan and New York: St. Martin's, 1983); and Tanya Basok and Robert J. Brym, "Soviet-Jewish emigration and resettlement in the 1990s: An overview" in Tanya Basok and Robert J. Brym (eds.), *Soviet-Jewish Emigration and Resettlement in the 1990s* (Toronto: York Lanes Press, York University, 1991), xi-xxii. Also useful was Laurie P. Salitan, *Politics and Nationality in Contemporary Soviet-Jewish Emigration, 1968-89* (New York: St. Martin's, 1992).

2   Data sources for 1971-1991: "Immigration data—1991", in *Yehudei brit hamoatsot* (The Jews of the Soviet Union), vol. 15, 1992, 188; for 1992: Sidney Heitman, "Jewish emigration from the former USSR in 1992", unpublished paper (Fort Collins CO: Department of History, Colorado State University, 1993). The 1993 data are projected from figures for the first ten months of the year. I estimate 1993 arrivals in countries other than Israel and the USA at about 15,000.

3   Igor Bestuzhev-Lada, "Social problems of the Soviet way of life", *Novy mir,* no. 7, 1976, 215.

4   "Kosygin on reunion of families and national equality (1966)" in Benjamin Pinkus (ed.), *The Soviet Government and the Jews 1948-1967* (Cambridge UK: Cambridge University Press, 1984), 78.

5   In addition, under the terms of the Soviet-Polish Repatriation Agreement (1957-59), about 14,000 Jews had been permitted to return to their native Poland.

6   Robert O. Freedman, "Soviet Jewry and Soviet-American relations" in Robert O. Freedman (ed.), *Soviet Jewry in the Decisive Decade, 1971-80* (Durham, NC: Duke University Press, 1984), 38-67; "Soviet Jewry as a factor in Soviet-Israeli relations" in Robert O. Freedman (ed.), *Soviet Jewry in the 1980s: The Politics of Anti-Semitism and Emigration and the Dynamics of Resettlement* (Durham NC: Duke University Press, 1989), 61-96; Marshall I. Goldman, "Soviet-American trade and Soviet Jewish emigration: Should a policy change be made by the American Jewish community?" in Robert O. Freedman (ed.), *Soviet Jewry in the 1980s . . .* , 141-59.

7   Gary Bertsch, "US-Soviet trade: The question of leverage", *Survey,* vol. 25, no. 2, 1980, 66-80.

8   Richard Lowenthal, "East-West *détente* and the future of Soviet Jewry", *Soviet Jewish Affairs*, vol. 3, no. 1, 1973, 24.

9   Brym, "Soviet Jewish emigration . . . ". The relationship beyond 1987 is not known because the analysis has not been updated.

10 Zaslavsky and Brym, 49-51, 121-2; Zvi Gitelman, "Soviet Jewish emigrants: Why are they choosing America?", *Soviet Jewish Affairs*, vol. 7, no. 1, 1977, 31-46.

11 At the time, some commentators argued that the Soviets cut the emigration rate in the 1980s because many Jews started using Israeli exit visas to leave Russia but then "dropped out" and went elsewhere. Presumably, that practice undermined the pretext that Jews were permitted to leave for purposes of family reunification. The Soviets allegedly feared that non-Jews might get the idea that emigration for reasons other than family unification was possible. They therefore virtually stopped the outflow of Jews. See, for example, Zvi Alexander, "Jewish emigration from the USSR in 1980", *Soviet Jewish Affairs,* vol. 11, no. 2, 1981, 3-21; Zvi Nezer, "Jewish emigration from the USSR in 1981-82", *Soviet Jewish Affairs,* vol. 12, no. 3, 1982, 3-17. The trouble with this argument is that it fits the facts poorly. Thus the Soviets refused to allow direct Moscow-Tel Aviv flights, an action inconsistent with their alleged desire to stop the westward flow of Jewish emigrants. Between 1979 and 1981 the rate of emigration rose most in precisely those Soviet cities with the highest proportion of emigrants headed to countries other than Israel. And in general there was a statistically significant *positive* correlation between the emigration rate and the proportion of emigrants headed to countries other than Israel throughout the period 1971-87. See Brym, "The changing rate . . . "; "Soviet-Jewish emigration . . . ".

12 Arkady N. Shevchenko, *Breaking with Moscow* (New York: Alfred A. Knopf, 1985), 261.

13 Murray Feshbach, "The Soviet Union: Population trends and dilemmas", *Population Bulletin,* vol. 37, no. 3, 1982, 1-45; Alexander J. Motyl, *Will the Non-Russians Rebel? State, Ethnicity, and Stability in the USSR* (Ithaca and London: Cornell University Press, 1987), 158-9.

14 Peter Reddaway, "Policy towards dissent since Khrushchev" in T. H. Rigby, Archie Brown and Peter Reddaway (eds.), *Authority, Power and Policy in the USSR: Essays Dedicated to Leonard Shapiro* (London: Macmillan, 1980), 186.

15 "Miscellaneous reports", *Chronicle of Current Events,* no. 52, 1980 [1979]), 129.

16 Theodore Friedgut, "Soviet anti-Zionism and antisemitism—Another cycle", *Soviet Jewish Affairs,* vol. 14, no. 1, 1984, 6.

17 "Soviet anti-semitism said to be ceasing", *Canadian Jewish News,* 20 August 1987.

18 Vladimir G. Kostakov, "Employment: Deficit or surplus?", *Kommunist,* no. 2, 1987, 78-89; "Cutback", *Pravda,* 4 March 1988. Fear of a brain drain is still expressed in some circles today. See, for example, Irena Orlova, "A sketch of the migration and refugee situation in Russia", *Refuge,* vol. 13, no. 2, 1993, 19-22.

19 Robert J. Brym, "The emigration potential of Czechoslovakia, Hungary, Lithuania, Poland and Russia: Recent survey results", *International Sociology,* vol. 7, no. 4, 1992, 387-95. The Western desire to promote Soviet emigration also weakened when potential migrants from Central and South America, southeast Asia and elsewhere began making loud and legitimate claims on the Western immigration system.

20 Gregg A. Beyer, "The evolving United States response to Soviet-Jewish emigration" in Tanya Basok and Robert J. Brym (eds.), *Soviet-Jewish Emi-*

gration and Resettlement in the 1990s, 105-39.

21 Roberta Cohen, "Israel's problematic absorption of Soviet Jews" in Tanya Basok and Robert J. Brym (eds.), *Soviet-Jewish Emigration and Resettlement in the 1990s*, 67-89.

22 Sidney Heitman, "Jewish emigration . . . ".

23 Michal Bodemann, "A renaissance of Germany Jewry?", paper presented at a conference on "The Reemergence of Jewish Culture in Germany", University of Toronto, 6-7 May 1993.

24 Recall that I weighted my sample so that, effectively, it consists of 54.5 per cent Muscovites, 33.2 per cent Kievans and only 12.3 per cent Minskers.

25 In the October 1992 survey I conducted with Andrei Degtyarev in Moscow there were only 23 Jewish respondents, of whom 5 (22 per cent) expressed the desire to emigrate. This is a small sub-sample and one should not read too much into the results. Nonetheless, the fact that 22 per cent of the 535 Moscow Jews in the survey conducted with Ryvkina (weighted n) also expressed the desire to emigrate should increase one's confidence in my findings. Compare Table 5.6, panel 1, with Robert J. Brym and Andrei Degtyarev, "Who wants to leave Moscow for the West? Results of an October 1992 survey", *Refuge,* vol. 13, no. 2, 1993, 24, Table 2. As this book went to press I learned that a survey recently conducted in Russia by Vladimir Shapiro, President of the Jewish Scientific Centre in Moscow, found that a third of Russian Jews wish to emigrate. This is consistent with my findings. The poll surveyed 1,300 Jews in Moscow, St Petersburg and Yekaterinburg. See Natasha Singer, "Poll: Jews staying in Russia", *Forward*, 13 August 1993.

26 Rozalina Ryvkina, "Value conflicts of Russian Jews and their social types", unpublished paper, Moscow, 1992.

27 A large random sample for a 1990 survey in ten republics of the USSR happened to include thirty-four Jews, a fifth of them from Georgia and none from Moscow or Leningrad. When the respondents were asked whether they would like to emigrate permanently, 71 per cent of the Jews said "yes". Note, however, that the sample of Jews is tiny and skewed towards regions with high rates of emigration. The survey was, moreover, conducted during the period of panic emigration. See Lev Gudkov and Alex Levinson, *Attitudes Toward Jews in the Soviet Union: Public Opinion in Ten Republics* (New York: The American Jewish Committee, 1992), 26-7.

28 For example, the USA is apparently planning to implement a new policy allowing people from the former Soviet republics with refugee status only one year to emigrate. This may speed up the pace of departure for some people with refugee status but it may force others to choose to go to Israel and still others not to leave at all. See "One-year limit on US refugee status for ex-USSR", *Monitor: Digest of News and Analysis from Soviet Successor States,* vol. 4, no. 25, 30 July/ 6 August 1993), 1.

29 Natan Sharansky, "The greatest exodus", *The New York Times Magazine*, 2 February 1992.

30 I note that the 1993 Israel budget proposal, tabled in 1992, predicted 154,000 CIS immigrants in 1993. A 1993 Israeli Treasury economic assessment paper lowered the figure to 80,000, but predicted 120,000 CIS immigrants per

year starting in 1994. Based on actual figures for the first ten months of 1993, I project 70,000 CIS immigrants for 1993. See Government of Israel, "The State Budget for 1993: Submitted to the Thirteenth Knesset" (Jerusalem: Government Printer, 1992) (in Hebrew), 114; "Surplus loan guarantees", *Canadian Jewish News*, 17 June 1993, 46.

31   I coded an eighth option ("I do not wish to leave Russia [Ukraine, Belarus]") as missing because in retrospect it seemed simply a restatement of the question. It received only thirty-two responses.

32   Eighteen respondents who said they planned to emigrate but were unsure which country they would go to were coded as missing. It did not make sense to standardize and add the two items because there were 1,000 valid responses for question 74 and only 288 valid responses for question 82. Instead I conducted a regression analysis on each item separately and determined that virtually the same predictors operated on each one and did so in the same direction and with similar magnitudes. This justifies combining the two items.

6 Between East and West

PATTERNS OF ACCOMMODATION

In the year 2000 fewer than half a million Jews will remain in the territory of the former USSR. What was the largest Jewish community in the world in 1900 will constitute less than 4 per cent of world Jewry at the end of the century. The Jews who remain will for the most part be old, highly assimilated and dwindling quickly in number. Already in 1988-9 about 37 per cent of the Jews in the USSR were 60 years of age or older. The total fertility rate was 1.6 children per Jewish woman—24 per cent below the rate needed to replace the population even in the absence of any net out-migration. Half of all marriages were to non-Jews and that rate was increasing over time. Given that the younger and more Jewish Jews are the most likely to emigrate, and that they are continuing to do so in large numbers, one cannot possibly be optimistic about the prospects for the Jewish community in the CIS in the next century.[1]

Meanwhile, the Jews who still find themselves in the CIS seek to adapt as best they can, to work out various patterns of accommodation to the circumstances of their existence. The former USSR comprises fifteen more or less loosely connected states of high anxiety. For each geographical, class and ethnic group in the region, these times of trouble are expressed in a particular form which depends on the group's history and social structure. For the Jews, the general anxiety is most conspicuously expressed as a series of tensions between the Slavic world, the West and Israel. These tensions have been evident throughout my examination of Jewish patterns of identification, perceptions of antisemitism and migration plans. The strains are also apparent in my respondents' general values and political preferences.

Consider in that connection Table 6.1. Respondents were asked whether they regard a whole range of values as very important, important or not important—being successful in business, having a professional career, being part of a good family, enjoying good health, commanding the respect of others, being a leader, participating in making important

Table 6.1
Migration Plans by General Values and Political Preferences (in per cent)

	average	migration plans		
		non-emigrants (n=572)	ambi-valents (n=141)	West-bound (n=191)	Israel-bound (n=78)

value ("very important" minus "not important")

	average	non-emigrants (n=572)	ambi-valents (n=141)	West-bound (n=191)	Israel-bound (n=78)
q152-health	85	86	76	86	87
q151-family	73	74	75	75	67
*q153-respect	49	[51]	{ 38}	50	47
*q154-independence	44	44	38	[51]	{ 29}
*q150-profession	- 8	{-15}	[12]	- 1	- 9
*q157-help Russia, etc.	-17	[- 8]	-29	-32	{-34}
*q149-business	-38	{-50}	[-15]	-20	-32
*q156-imp. decisions	-40	{-44}	-37	[-33]	{-44}
*q155-be leader	-68	{-72}	-64	[-58]	-69
*q158-be in Israel	-75	{-92}	-72	-83	[36]

q159-era preference

	average	non-emigrants	ambi-valents	West-bound	Israel-bound
*Yeltsin	33	34	[45]	{ 23}	43
<1917	29	25	35	39	28
Brezhnev	20	21	13	18	21
Khrushchev	7	8	3	5	3
Gorbachev	6	6	3	11	2
Lenin	3	5	0	1	1
Stalin	2	2	1	2	2
total		101	100	99	100

q160-government preference

	average	non-emigrants	ambi-valents	West-bound	Israel-bound
*business	51	{ 47}	[63]	55	52
*same as current	24	[28]	{ 15}	18	27
*directors	13	[14]	[14]	13	{ 4}
Communist	4	4	3	5	0
*religious	3	{ 2}	3	4	[10]
military	3	3	0	3	2
national-patriotic	3	2	2	2	5
total		100	100	100	100

*q161-Western influence ("not enough" minus "too much")

14	{- 5}	[44]	23	41

Table 6.1 (cont'd)
Migration Plans by General Values and Political Preferences (in per cent)

Note: Items preceded by an asterisk indicate statistically significant differences between maximum and minimum row values at the .05 probability level. For those items, highest row values are enclosed in brackets ([]) and lowest row values are enclosed in braces ({ }). The maximum number of valid responses is shown above (n=x) but the exact number varies slightly from question to question. Percentages do not necessarily add up to 100 due to rounding.

decisions, enjoying personal independence, helping Russia (or Ukraine or Belarus) and being in Israel. They were also asked in which era they would prefer to live in if they could choose—that of Yeltsin, Gorbachev, Brezhnev, Khrushchev, Stalin, Lenin or the period before 1917. They were asked what sort of government they would prefer to see in power in Russia (or Ukraine or Belarus)—the same as now or a government led by entrepreneurs, directors of large (mainly state-owned) enterprises, Communists, religious figures, military personnel or so-called national-patriotic forces. Finally, they were asked whether there was too much, enough or not enough Western influence on Russian (or Ukrainian or Belarusian) culture and traditions. Table 6.1 cross-classifies their responses to these questions with their migration plans.

From the first column of Table 6.1 we immediately learn that, overall, the Jews of Moscow, Kiev and Minsk form a pro-Western group who prefer the Yeltsin era over all other periods of Soviet and pre-Soviet history but who would like to see their government led by entrepreneurs more than by any other category of the population. Clearly, the respondents are champions of liberal-democratic and capitalist reform. Like most people in most times and places, they value good health and family above all else. But the fact that they value respect and personal independence so much more than being a leader or being responsible for making important decisions may be regarded as a response to recent Soviet and post-Soviet history. Having suffered countless indignities and dependencies in the Soviet era, they now cherish respect and personal independence. But having survived for so long by laying low and quietly fitting in, they are still cautious about standing out as important decision-makers and especially as leaders.

This general characterization masks interesting dissimilarities between people with different emigration plans. These dissimilarities are brought into relief by comparing columns two to five in Table 6.1. Differences between some maximum and minimum row values are large enough that we can be 95 per cent sure they are not due to chance. Those items are preceded by an asterisk. Their high values are enclosed in square brackets ([ ]) and their low values in braces ({ }).

Compared to those who plan to emigrate, respondents who intend to stay in Russia, Ukraine or Belarus may be characterized as pro-Slavic conformists.[2] Why pro-Slavic? Because they comprise the only group in my sample who tend to believe that there is too much Western influence on Russian (or Ukrainian or Belarusian) culture and traditions. They are, moreover, the most inclined to believe in the importance of helping Russia (or Ukraine or Belarus) and the least inclined to think that it is important to be in Israel. Why conformist? Because they are anything but innovators. Of all four groups, they tend least to value professional and business life and are least inclined to be leaders. They (along with respondents who plan to move to Israel) are also least interested in being involved in making important decisions. True to form, they tend more than members of any other group to support the political status quo. Yet they demonstrate a certain insecurity in so far as they need respect from others more than the members of any other group. In short, they are survivors, and in the socio-historical context in which they find themselves that means being accommodationists *par excellence*.

The respondents who plan on moving to the Jewish state may be characterized as pro-Israel conformists. They are least likely to want to help Russia (or Ukraine or Belarus) and, of course, most likely to want to be in Israel. They tend least to value personal independence and they are tied with pro-Slavic conformists in their lack of desire to become involved in making important decisions. It seems that a small minority of them have an extraordinarily strong attachment to Israel and/ or an exceedingly bitter attitude towards Russia (or Ukraine or Belarus). Thus 15 per cent of them —far more than in any other group—would like to see a government led by religious or national-patriotic forces in Russia (or Ukraine or Belarus). Presumably, like Bakunin, they believe that the worse the better; such governments would in all likelihood force all Jews out and, given the limit on immigration to the USA, that means a huge boon to Israel.

Respondents who are unsure about whether they will emigrate and those who plan to emigrate to countries other than Israel resemble one another in terms of the attitudes measured here. However, they both contrast sharply with the two conformist groups. They thus display an intermediate level of Jewishness compared to the other groups and they are significantly more likely than the others to be innovators in their day-to-day lives.[3]

Respondents who plan to emigrate to countries other than Israel value being leaders, making important decisions and enjoying personal independence more than the members of any other group. Interestingly, however, they also display a high level of nostalgia. They are the least inclined to be happy about living in the Yeltsin era and the most inclined to wish they could have lived in the period before 1917.

The responses of the ambivalents—those who are unsure about their migration plans—suggest that they value autonomy and industry more highly than do other respondents. They thus care least about other people's opinions in the sense that they value the respect of others least. They are the most likely to want more Western influence on Russian (or Ukrainian or Belarusian) traditions and culture. They value their professional and business lives more than any other group of respondents. They are the staunchest supporters of the Yeltsin era but they are also the most eager for political change. Specifically, they are most inclined to support a government led by entrepreneurs.

Figure 6.1
Four Adaptation/Rejection Strategies

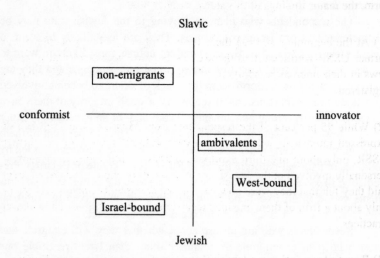

The four patterns of responses that I have just outlined are summarized graphically in Figure 6.1. The Figure suggests that each group is characterized by what might be called a different adaptation-rejection syndrome, a different mechanism for resolving the tensions that characterize

Jewish life in the CIS today. This is most obvious in terms of their different migration plans but it is also clear from the distribution of their attitudes towards issues that have little direct bearing on those plans. The pro-Slavic conformists tend to adapt by assimilating and blending quietly into their societies, rejecting many types of activities and patterns of association that would single them out for notice. The pro-Israel conformists are also keen not to stand out but they reject their country and, in some cases, hope that their country will reject all the Jews. Both the ambivalents and the respondents who are bound for the West adapt by innovation, not conformity. They emphasize eagerness to take initiative and to excel in business and professional life while rejecting the status quo, yearning either for a political regime that will be led by entrepreneurs or, less realistically, for a romantic era long past.

SUMMARY OF MAIN FINDINGS

My analysis has netted some results that are obvious, some that are not self-evident and some that are surprising and may provoke controversy. In point form, the major findings of this study are as follows:

(1) At the beginning of 1993 there were roughly 1,144,000 people in the former USSR who identified themselves as Jews, who were registered as Jews in their internal passports or who had at least one parent who was so registered.

(2) While 95 per cent of the respondents from Moscow, Kiev and Minsk expressed interest in witnessing a Jewish cultural revival in the former USSR, only about one-third expressed interest in remaining or becoming personally involved in the Jewish community, only about a quarter of them said they felt that they were now part of that community and an average of only about a fifth of them engaged in various Jewish religious and cultural practices.

(3) Respondents feel more Jewish if they have a strong Jewish upbringing, if they plan on emigrating, if their mother, spouse or father was or is registered as a Jew in his or her internal passport, if they have experienced antisemitism and fear it, and if they live in smaller peripheral centres (Minsk) as opposed to larger central cities (Moscow).

(4) In Moscow, a relatively liberal city by CIS standards, negative attitudes towards Jews are widespread by North American standards. For example, 18 per cent of Muscovites agree or are inclined to agree that there exists a global "Zionist" conspiracy against Russia and another 24 per cent are undecided. This does not, however, suggest that Jews are in imminent physical danger.

(5) In Moscow negative attitudes towards Jews are more widespread among older people, low-income earners and non-Russians.

(6) Compared to other republics of the former USSR, negative attitudes towards Jews are low in Russia and Ukraine but high in Belarus.[4]

(7) Nearly four-tenths of Jews in Moscow, Kiev and Minsk regard popular hostility as the main source of antisemitism today. A quarter of the respondents mention nationalist organizations, another quarter regard state policy and a tenth view anti-Jewish articles in the press as the taproot of anti-Jewish feeling.

(8) These perceptions vary from city to city. Muscovites regard organized group antisemitism as more of a problem than do Jews in the other two cities. Kievans are most inclined to think that popular hostility against Jews is highly problematic. Minskers are most likely to view the state apparatus as the main source of antisemitism in their country.

(9) While over 90 per cent of respondents in Moscow, Kiev and Minsk believe that antisemitism exists in their respective countries, 15 per cent more Muscovites than Kievans and Minskers believe that pogroms are likely or certain to break out. Ten per cent more Minskers than Kievans and Muscovites have personally experienced antisemitism. And Jews in Moscow perceive by far the largest decline in antisemitism since the rise of Gorbachev.

(10) Nearly a third of Jews in Moscow, Kiev and Minsk express a great deal of apprehension about antisemitism. Heightened fear is most strongly associated with witnessing antisemitism in the mass media, being a woman, having a strong Jewish identity, lacking confidence in one's future and being in one's thirties, forties or fifties.

(11) Extremely rough projections suggest that over 480,000 Jews will emigrate from the USSR between 1994 and 1999. Between 204,000 and 275,000 of them will go to Israel. Between 276,000 and 368,000 of them will go elsewhere.

(12) Nearly six-tenths of respondents with emigration plans said that they planned to emigrate mainly for economic reasons, a third for reasons having to do with political instability and ethnic conflict, and fewer than a tenth for purposes of family reunification.

(13) In contrast, nearly half the respondents said that cultural affinity roots them in their country, over a quarter said they were tied to their country by family and friendship connections and over 10 per cent mentioned economic activities as the most important ties to their country.

(14) About 30 per cent of respondents planning to emigrate to countries other than Israel said that they did not want to go to Israel because it was culturally alien to them. Another 30 per cent said that poor job prospects dissuaded them from choosing Israel as a destination. Twenty per cent of the potential emigrants said they did not wish to go to Israel because they had few friends and/ or relatives there and 14 per cent said they did not want to go because of the Arab-Israeli conflict and the threat of war. About 30 per cent of respondents planning to go the West said that they would go to Israel if they could secure a job comparable to the one they currently hold.

A FINAL WORD ON METHOD

In October 1944 Churchill met with representatives of the Polish government-in-exile in an attempt to convince them to cede Poland's eastern territories to Russia, as Stalin demanded. When Stanislaw Mikolajczyk, the Prime Minister of the "London Poles", said that Polish public opinion would not accept the loss, Churchill shot back "What is public opinion? The right to be crushed!"[5]

In one sense, public opinion matters little, as Churchill clearly understood. It is often shaped by large impersonal forces and at least some of it is an ephemera of everyday life—the raw material for the proverbial newspaper that shouts today's headlines but that tomorrow will be used as wrapping-up paper. From that point of view, a survey is outdated, if not irrelevant, the moment it is conducted. When, in addition, it represents the opinions of only part of the population of interest one is obliged to ask whether its value is out of all proportion to the effort expended in executing it.

I readily admit to the shortcomings implied by Churchill's jab, although not to the conclusions one may hastily draw from it. Yeltsin, Kravchuk, Shushkevich and their regimes now appear to be muddling through—barely. They could, however, be overthrown, much to the serious detriment of Jewish cultural and political freedom in the region.[6] Similarly, a change in American immigration regulations or a further deterioration of the Israeli economy would have serious and direct consequences for the Jewish community of the former Soviet Union. Emigration plans, cultural practice and much else would be bound to alter under such pressure.

Eventually, public opinion would follow suit, at least to a degree. In the long run most people adapt to changed circumstances and rationalize their adaptations by altering their views, even their self-conceptions. One must be careful, however, not to exaggerate the plasticity of public opinion. Some views change from day to day, like the popularity of prime ministers and presidents. Other attitudes are more profound and resist change. Stalin did not, after all, crush the Polish desire for independence.

I believe that many of the attitudes tapped by my survey are deeply held and that the results therefore tell us something enduringly important about the Jews of Moscow, Kiev and Minsk. True, in a couple of places I made some shaky assumptions in order to force my data to say something about the size of the entire Jewish population of the former USSR and their emigration plans. But taken together, doubts about the relevance of public opinion in the face of overpowering circumstances, about the obduracy of some attitudes in the face of changed conditions and about the representativeness of my sample for purposes of making some generalizations suggest to me the need for more surveys, not fewer. Broader-based surveys will yield sounder inferences. Polls taken under a variety of social, economic and political circumstances will give a better sense of how Jews in the former USSR may be expected to act under a multiplicity of conditions, including, if the worse comes to the worst, the exercise of brute force.

In the field of what used to be called Sovietology, and more narrowly among students of Jews in the former USSR, there are few sociologists and many historians who are sceptical of the utility of surveys. The historians inventively stitch together documentary evidence, speculate imaginatively and employ a deep appreciation of Russian, Jewish and other cultures to arrive at explanations and understandings of their subject matter. I do not wish to denigrate the importance of their research. On the contrary, I admire it greatly and have in places relied on it heavily. Based partly on the record of some Sovietologists and students of Jews in the former USSR, however, I strongly believe that documentary investigation, ingenious speculation and deep cultural understanding are often fallible and need to be supplemented by systematically observing, counting and generalizing from the patterns of belief and action tracked by survey and other quantitative data. From my point of view, some scholars in the area build their arguments on meagre evidentiary foundations. When challenged, they sometimes sound like the frustrated *chasid* who, when asked to prove that God actually caused the Red Sea to part, could only extend his arms and indignantly blurt the virtually untranslatable *"Nu du zayst doch!"* (roughly: "Well, you can see!"). Here I have offered another basis for understanding, a basis with its own strengths and its own shortcomings. Documentary investigation, clever speculation and the understanding of deep cultural meaning are important. So are numeracy and the sociological method.

NOTES

1   Mordechai Altshuler, "Socio-demographic profile of Moscow Jews", *Jews and Jewish Topics in the Soviet Union and Eastern Europe*, 3 (16), 1991, 28-9; Mark Tolts, "Jewish marriages in the USSR: A demographic analysis", *East European Jewish Affairs*, vol. 22, no. 2, 1993, 8-9, 17.
2   Note the basis of comparison. The rubric would hardly make sense if the respondents were being compared to a sample of Slavs. An analogous argument holds for the names I use to characterize the other groups. Note also that I initially divided the respondents who did not plan to emigrate into those who ranked in the top and bottom half of my scale of Jewishness. I found no significant differences between the two subgroups in the values examined here. I repeated this procedure after dividing non-emigrants into those who ranked in the bottom two-thirds and the top third of the scale of Jewishness but still found no significant differences. I therefore decided to lump all non-emigrants together.
3   Table 6.1 shows that there is a statistically insignificant difference between the two groups in terms of how much value they place on helping Russia (or Ukraine or Belarus). However, the ambivalents value being in Israel significantly more than do those bound for destinations other than Israel despite their being less Jewish than the latter respondents (as we learned from Table 5.6). This suggests just how ambivalent they are.
4   This generalization is based on an inspection and partial re-analysis of Gudkov's and Levinson's 1992 data.
5   Quoted in Martin Gilbert, *Churchill: A Life* (London: Minerva, 1991), 798.
6   I. V. Chernenko and M. M. Zakhvatkin, "The fascism-socialism dichotomy from the point of view of catastrophe theory", *Rossiysky monitor: Arkhiv sovremennoy politiki,* no. 1, 1992, 92-3; Galina Starovoitova, "Weimar Russia?", *Journal of Democracy,* vol. 4, no. 3, 1993, 106-9.

Appendix A
Methodological Notes

Table A.1 lists the surnames used to select the sample (see Chapter 1 for details).

Table A.2 gives frequency distributions for the basic socio-demographic characteristics of the people in the sample. Comparative data on the Moscow Jewish population according to the 1989 census are given where available.

Table A.3 gives frequency distributions for the sex, age and educational level of nonrespondents, i.e., people who were contacted but who declined to take part in the survey. Data were obtained from other household members. The distributions are very similar to those for respondents. This strongly suggests that nonresponse bias is not a problem in this survey.

As a check on the validity of responses, interviewers were asked after each interview to rank the respondents on a scale of 1 to 5, where 1 indicates that the respondent appeared "very open" in answering questions and 5 indicates that he or she seemed "very closed". The average score was 1.9, which suggests that in general respondents felt comfortable during the interview and gave frank and honest answers.

Interviewers were also asked to indicate which questions, if any, the respondents found difficult to answer. By far the most difficult set of questions concerned the issue of who benefited from the notion that antisemitism existed in their country (q141-q148). An average of 4.7 per cent of respondents found these eight questions difficult to answer. That figure is too low to be of concern.

Table A.1
The Most Common Jewish Surnames in Russia, Ukraine and Belarus (n=405)

Abramov	Bronshteyn	Fish	Igolnik
Abramovich	Bunimovich	Fisher	Ilinets
Abramson		Fishman	Ioffe
Agranovich	Dagman	Fogel	Itenberg
Akselrod	Dashevsky	Fradkin	Itskovich
Altman	Davidovich	Frayberg	Izakson
Altshuler	Davidson	Frayerman	Izrael
Aptekman	Deller	Frid	Izraelson
Arev	Deych	Fridlin	Izrailson
Aranovich	Diligensky	Fridlyand	Izrailev
Aronov	Dimerman	Fridman	
Aronson	Diner	Frishman	Kagan
Arshavsky	Dintan	Fuks	Kagansky
Asbel	Dipman	Funtik	Kalmanovich
Ashkinazi	Domansky	Furman	Kantor
Averbakh	Domnich	Futerman	Kantorovich
Averbukh	Dorfman		Kaplan
Ayzekovich	Dunaevsky	Garfunkel	Kaplun
Ayzenberg	Dverin	Gelman	Kaplunovich
Ayzenshtat	Dvorkin	Gelner	Karpachevsky
	Dvoskin	Gerd	Karpelson
Basin	Dymersky	Gerdt	Karsik
Batkin	Dymshits	Gershenson	Kats
Belenky		Gershikovich	Katsen
Benevich	Fakhzon	Gershuni	Katsman
Beninson	Faktor	Gerts	Katsnelson
Berelson	Faktorovich	Gilevich	Katsner
Berg	Fayn	Gilinsky	Kazakevich
Berger	Faynberg	Gitelman	Kaziner
Bergman	Faynleyb	Glozman	Khashis
Berkovich	Fayntikh	Gofman	Khaymovich
Berlyand	Fegin	Goltsman	Khenkin
Berngart	Feldbeyn	Golod	Kheyfits
Bernshteyn	Feldman	Gorfinkel	Kheynman
Beylin	Feltsman	Gorodetsky	Khidekel
Blyum	Felsot	Gozman	Khmelnitsky
Blyumin	Fiks	Gurevich	Khotinsky
Blyumkin	Finkel	Gurvich	Khurgin
Braude	Finkelshteyn		Kleyman

Table A.1 (cont'd)
The Most Common Jewish Surnames in Russia, Ukraine and Belarus (n=405)

Kleyner	Lurie	Nosonovsky	Ravich
Kofman	Lyublinsky	Noyberg	Ravichbakh
Kogan		Noyman	Ravikovich
Kon	Magaliv	Nudelman	Rekhman
Korman	Maltser	Nudman	Revzin
Krasik	Malkin		Rivers
Kreymer	Malkind	Paperny	Roginsky
Kugel	Margulis	Pekarsky	Rossin
Kugelman	Markel	Pekelis	Rotenfeld
Kunin	Markovich	Pelman	Rotman
Kuperman	Matizen	Perchik	Rovinsky
Kupershteyn	Mayer	Perelman	Roytman
Kushner	Maykin	Peres	Royzman
Kushnerovich	Mayminas	Pevzner	Rozenbaum
	Mayzel	Peysakhovich	Rozenkrants
Lebenzon	Mazo	Pinkhusov	Rozin
Lebin	Meerovich	Pinsker	Rozman
Lebind	Melman	Pinus	Rozovsky
Lefner	Meltser	Plavnik	Rubin
Lerner	Men	Pliner	Rubinchik
Levin	Meyer	Plotkin	Rubinshteyn
Levinson	Meyerkhold	Polyansky	Rukhman
Levintov	Meyerson	Ponizovsky	Rumanovsky
Levit	Milner	Portnov	Ruvinsky
Levitin	Minkin	Portnoy	Ryvkin
Levitsky	Mirkin	Prezent	Ryvlin
Leybkind	Mordkovich	Prigozhin	
Leybov	Mordukhovich	Prilutsky	Sabler
Leybzon		Pritsker	Sakhnovich
Leyfman	Nakhamkin	Pulkin	Saminsky
Leykin	Natan	Pyatigorsky	Sandler
Libin	Natanovich		Seminsky
Lifshits	Natanson	Rabikovich	Shapiro
Likhtenshteyn	Nayshul	Rabin	Shatskin
Lipkin	Nedlin	Rabinovich	Shatsman
Lokshin	Neginsky	Rakovshchik	Shekhtman
Loshinker	Nekhamkin	Ram	Sher
Lukatsky	Neyman	Rappoport	Shereshevsky
Lukhman	Neymark	Rashragovich	Sherman

Table A.1 (cont'd)
The Most Common Jewish Surnames in Russia, Ukraine and Belarus (n=405)

Sheylin	Strokovsky	Volfson
Sheynis	Svecharnik	Volodarsky
Shifman	Sverdlik	Volynsky
Shifrin	Sverdlov	Vorovich
Shifris	Sviridov	Vorovsky
Shikhman		Vortman
Shilman	Tabger	
Shkolnik	Tomarkin	Zak
Shmulevich	Traber	Zakher
Shmurak	Trakhtenberg	Zakhoder
Shnirman	Trakhtenbrod	Zakhtser
Shor	Tubman	Zaks
Shpirman	Tsadik	Zaltsman
Shpulman	Tsetlin	Zalmanov
Shteynberg	Tseydlin	Zaskovich
Shulman	Tsimbal	Zaslavsky
Shusterman	Tsimbalist	Zeldin
Shustik	Tsimernan	Zelkin
Sigal	Tsodik	Zelman
Simanovich	Tsyperovich	Zelmanovsky
Simkin		Zeltser
Sliozberg	Valdman	Zeltsin
Slobodinsky	Varshavsky	Zeltesan
Slobodkin	Vasserman	Zelnik
Slonim	Vatermakhen	Zenkevich
Smidovich	Vatsman	Ziglin
Smigal	Vayl	Zikherman
Smolkin	Vaynshteyn	Zilberg
Smorgonsky	Vayserman	Zilberovich
Smorodinsky	Vaysman	Zilbershteyn
Solomonik	Veber	Ziselts
Solomonov	Vesler	Ziskind
Sorin	Veykher	Zolotar
Sternin	Veysman	Zorin
Stiskin	Vilner	Zul
Stokovsky	Volf	Zusman

Table A.2
Frequency Distributions of Basic Sociodemographic Variables
(in per cent; n in parentheses)

q7-sex			Moscow education (aged 15+)	
male	50		preprimary	1
female	50		primary	2
total	100	(1,001)	incom. secondary	6
male/female sex ratio= 1.00			secondary gen.	12
Moscow m/f sex ratio = 1.14			secondary voc.	14
			incom. higher	4
			higher	60
q8-age			total	99
18-29	18			
30-39	15			
40-49	22		q10-marital status	
50-59	28		married	69
60-90	17		never mar	15
total	100	(1,001)	sep div	10
average=46.5	s.d.=15.8		widow	7
			total	101 (1,000)
Moscow age				
0- 9	5		q11-family size	
10-19	6		1	9
20-29	8		2	26
30-39	11		3	31
40-49	14		4	22
50-59	18		5	10
60+	40		6	2
total	102		7	1
			total	101 (1,000)
			average=3.1	s.d.=1.3
q9-education				
7-8	1			
9-11	13		q12-number of children	
tech/prof	4		0	23
tekhnikum	14		1	43
some univ	62		2	31
phd	5		3	3
dr sci	1		total	100 (993)
total	100	(1,001)	average=1.1	s.d.=.8

Table A.2 (cont'd)
Frequency Distributions of Basic Sociodemographic Variables
(in per cent; n in parentheses)

q14-work status			Moscow occupation		
employed	67		white collar	85	
unemployed	3		blue collar	15	
homemaker	4		total	100	
retired	20				
student	6				
other	1		q29-total monthly income		
total	10	(1,000)	(in roubles)		
			0-5000	28	
q15-sector if employed			5001-10000	20	
state	70		10001-15000	16	
private	19		15001-20000	12	
both	11		20001-40000	16	
total	100	(663)	40000-1 mil	8	
			total	100	(1,001)
q17-occupation			average=23,425	s.d.=57,137	
scientist	8		median=13,800		
engineer	32				
teacher	8				
physician	5		q35-dwelling type		
lawyer	1		state flat	56	
manual	9		priv flat	39	
free profess	6		commun flat	2	
govt service	7		parents' flat	1	
govt admin	6		other	1	
entrepreneur	5		total	99	(997)
private manag	15				
total	102	(656)			

Source for Moscow data: Mordechai Altshuler, "Socio-demographic profile of Moscow Jews", *Jews and Jewish Topics in the Soviet Union and Eastern Europe*, 3 (16), 1991, 24-40.

Note: Due to weighting and missing cases, frequencies do not necessarily add up to 1,000 and percentages do not necessarily add up to 100.0.

Table A.3
Characteristics of Nonrespondents (in per cent; n in parentheses)

sex			education		
male	58		<7	0	
female	42		7-8	2	
total	100	(218)	9-11	12	
			tech/prof	5	
age			tekhnikum	9	
18-29	15		some univ	69	
30-39	10		phd	2	
40-49	23		dr sci	1	
50-59	28		total	100	(214)
60-90	23				
total	99	(213)			
average=48.9	s.d.=15.7				

Note: Due to weighting, the frequencies reported here differ slightly from the unweighted non-response frequency reported in Chapter 1 and percentages do not necessarily add up to 100.0.

Appendix B
The Questionnaire

1. Questionnaire ID number _____

PART A [INTERVIEW IDENTIFICATION INFORMATION. TO BE COM-
PLETED BY INTERVIEWER IMMEDIATELY BEFORE INTERVIEW IS CON-
DUCTED.]

2. Month_____ *[Specify 1-12]*

3. Day of Month_____ *[Specify 1-31]*

4. Time of Day_____ *[Specify 1-24]*

5. City_____ *[Specify 1-3, where 1=Moscow, 2=Kiev, 3=Minsk]*

PART B [SCREENING QUESTION. TO BE READ TO EACH RESPONDENT.]

Good evening. I am helping a group of sociologists in Moscow and Toronto conduct a public opinion poll on Jewish emigration from Russia. We would be very
grateful if you (or an adult member of your family) would answer our questionnaire.

I want to emphasize that your household was selected at random. All responses will be kept completely anonymous: we do not wish to ask you your name
and there is no way to connect your name with your responses. It will take about an
hour to answer our questions. You may refuse to answer any questions that you do
not wish to answer for whatever reason.

I would like to interview a person in your household eighteen years or older.
If you are not alone at home I'd like to interview the adult who had the most recent
birthday.

6. May I interview that person or you?

yes   no
1   2

[If "no" go to question 179.]

PART C [SOCIO-DEMOGRAPHIC QUESTIONS.]

7. *[Interviewer: indicate by observation whether respondent is a man or woman.]*

male   female
1   2

8. First, would you please tell me how old you are?
[Interviewer: specify figure.]

_____ years   99 don't know or refused

[If "under 18" say:] I am afraid that you are too young to participate in our survey. Thank you anyway for your willingness to help us, and good evening.

[Ask question 9 only for those who 18 or older.]

9. What level of schooling did you complete?

less than elementary school	elementary school (grades 7-8)	middle school (grades 9-11)	technical-professional school	teknikum
1	2	3	4	5

at least some university	Ph.D.	Doctor of Science (Full Professor)	don't know or refused
6	7	8	99

10. Are you married, never-married, separated or divorced, or widowed?

married	never married	separated or divorced	widowed	don't know or refused
1	2	3	4	99

11. How many people are in your family?
[Interviewer: Specify figure.]

_____ people   99 don't know or refused

12. How many children do you have?
[Interviewer: Specify figure.]

_____ children   99 don't know or refused

[Interviewer: Ask question 13 only for those who have children.]

13. How many of your children live abroad now?
[Interviewer: Specify figure.]

_____ children living abroad   99 don't know or refused

PART D [QUESTIONS ON SOCIO-ECONOMIC POSITION.]

**14. Which of the following best describes your present situation—
employed, unemployed, homemaker, retired, student, or other?**

employed	unemployed	homemaker	retired	student
1	2	3	4	5

other	don't know or refused
6	99

[Interviewer: Ask questions 15-27 only for "employed".]

**15. In which sector do you work—the state sector, the private sector, or in both
sectors?**

state sector	private sector	in both sectors	don't know or refused
1	2	3	99

[Interviewer: Ask question 16 only for employed in both sectors.]

**16. What about your main occupation—is it in the state sector, the private
sector or equally in both sectors?**

state sector	private sector	both sectors	don't know or refused
1	2	3	99

17. And what is your occupation?

scientist	engineer	teacher	physician	lawyer
1	2	3	4	5

manual worker	independendent worker (freelance writer, artist, etc.)		government administrator
6	7		8

employee in state organization	entrepreneur	employee in private organization	other	don't know or refused
9	10	11	12	99

18. What administrative (managerial) post do you hold?

director or deputy director of organization	head of department	professional
1	2	3

other post	none of the above	don't know or refused
4	5	99

19. Do you feel that you are satisfied or not satisfied with your work?

satisfied	not satisfied	don't know or refused
1	2	99

What features of your work do you like or not like?

[Interviewer: Specify 1=like, 2=don't like, 99=don't know or refused.]

20. wages (salary) _____

21. conditions of work _____

22. your relations with managers above _____

23. your relations with your colleagues _____

24. your post _____

25. opportunities for advancement _____

What if anything do you wish to change in your work?
[Interviewer: Specify: 1=wish to change, 2=don't wish to change, 99=don't know or refused.]

26. the organization you work for _____

27. your profession _____

28. How well off is your family in material terms? Please indicate your family's position on a five-point scale where "1" is very rich, "2" is rich, "3" is middle income, "4" is poor, "5" is very poor.

very rich	rich	middle-income	poor	very poor
1	2	3	4	5

don't know or refused
99

29. What is your total monthly income from all sources?
[Interviewer: Specify figure in roubles.]

_____ roubles   99 don't know or refused

Please indicate how many roubles of your total monthly income comes from each of the following sources:
[Interviewer: specify number of roubles from each source. If respondent does not have income from a source, specify "0".]

30. wages _____   99 don't know or refused

31. business profits _____ 99 don't know or refused

32. unemployment insurance _____   99 don't know or refused

33. pensions and stipends _____   99 don't know or refused

34. other _____   99 don't know or refused

35. What type of residence does your family occupy?

single state flat	single privately-owned flat		rooms in communal flat	place in hostel
1	2		3	4

parent's flat	rent a residence	other	don't know or refused	
5	6	7	99	

36. Please tell me which of the following items you own:
[Interviewer: Read options and ask respondent to indicate the items s/he owns.]

dacha	plot of land	car	video tape recorder	don't know or refused
1	2	3	4	99

37. Did you travel abroad in 1991-92?

yes	no	don't know or refused
1	2	99

38. In general, how do you feel about your standard of living--are you satisfied or dissatisfied?

satisfied	dissatisfied	don't know or refused
1	2	99

39. What do you think your standard of living is likely to be in the next 1-2 years--better, the same or worse?

better   the same   worse   don't know or refused
1   2   3   99

40. How do you feel about your current occupational position? Are you satisfied with it, or would you like to occupy a lower or higher position?

satisfied   would like   would like   don't know
with current higher   lower   or refused
position   position   position
1   2   3   99

41. Are conditions favourable to your obtaining a higher occupational position in your country?

yes   no   don't know or refused
1   2   99

PART E [QUESTIONS ABOUT THE ETHNIC COMPOSITION OF THE RESPONDENT'S FAMILY.]

I now want to ask you a few questions about your nationality and the nationality of your parents and spouse.

42. What is (or was) your father's nationality according to his passport?

Russian   Ukrainian   Belarusian   Jewish   other
1   2   3   4   5

don't know or refused
99

43. What is (or was) your mother's nationality according to her passport?

Russian   Ukrainian   Belarusian   Jewish   other
1   2   3   4   5

don't know or refused
99

44. What is (or was) your spouse's nationality according to his/ her passport?

Russian   Ukrainian   Belarusian   Jewish   other
1   2   3   4   5

have no spouse   don't know or refused
6   99

45. What is your nationality according to your passport?

Russian   Ukrainian   Belarusian   Jewish   other
1   2   3   4   5

don't know or refused
99

46. Did you ever change the nationality registration in your passport?

yes   no   don't know or refused
1   2   99

47. Some people identify with the nationality listed in their passport while others do not. With which nationality do you most closely identify?

Russian   Ukrainian   Belarusian   Jewish   other
1   2   3   4   6

Jewish and other simultaneously   other   don't know
                                                           or refused
5   6   99

[Interviewer: Ask questions 48-158 only for those who answered "Jewish" on questions 42, 43, 45 or 47, or "Jewish and other simultaneously" on question 47.]

PART F [JEWISH CULTURAL PRACTICE.]

48. I want to ask you a few questions about your Jewish cultural roots. First, thinking about your upbringing in your parents' home, would you say that your involvement in Jewish culture—that is, languages, religious customs and history—was great, moderate, weak or negligible?

great   moderate   weak   negligible   don't know
                                                          or refused
1   2   3   4   99

49. Do you speak Hebrew? If so, how well do you speak it—well, moderately well or poorly?

well   moderately   poorly   not at all   don't know
                                                          or refused
1   2   3   4   99

50. Do you speak Yiddish? If so, how well do you speak it--well, moderately well or poorly?

well	moderately	poorly	not at all	don't know or refused
1	2	3	4	99

[Interviewer: Ask questions 51-55 only for those who responded "well", "moderately" or "poorly" on questions 49 and 50.]

How do you use Hebrew or Yiddish in your everyday life? Do you often, occasionally or never read literature or the press, communicate in family, communicate with friends, communicate with Israelis, communicate in synagogue?

51. read literature or the press

often	occasionally	never	don't know or refused
1	2	3	99

52. communicate in family

often	occasionally	never	don't know or refused
1	2	3	99

53. communicate with friends

often	occasionally	never	don't know or refused
1	2	3	99

54. communicate with Israelis

often	occasionally	never	don't know or refused
1	2	3	99

55. communicate in synagogue

often	occasionally	never	don't know or refused
1	2	3	99

[Interviewer: Ask question 56 only for those who answered "don't know" on questions 49 and 50.]

56. Do you plan to learn Hebrew or Yiddish?

yes	no	don't know or refused
1	2	99

Please indicate whether you usually celebrate the following Jewish holidays:

57. Sabbath

yes	no	don't know or refused
1	2	99

58. Jewish New Year

yes	no	don't know or refused
1	2	99

59. Day of Atonement

yes	no	don't know or refused
1	2	99

60. Passover

yes	no	don't know or refused
1	2	99

61. How often do you visit synagogue--often, occasionally or never?

often	occasionally	never	don't know or refused
1	2	3	99

62. Do you think it is necessary to develop the Jewish religion in your country?

yes	no	don't know or refused
1	2	99

63. Do you participate in the work of any Jewish organizations?

yes	no	don't know or refused
1	2	99

64. Are you a member of any Jewish organizations—cultural, religious, political or social?

yes	no	don't know or refused
1	2	99

65. How often do you read the Jewish press—often, occasionally or never?

often	occasionally	never	don't know or refused
1	2	3	99

66. Do you think that a Jewish community exists in your country?

yes   no   don't know or refused
1   2   99

[Interviewer: Ask question 67 only for those who answered "yes" on question 66.]

67. Do you feel that you belong to the Jewish community?

yes   no   don't know or refused
1   2   99

68. How do you feel about your dealings with Jews--are they enough, too little or too much?

enough   too little   too much   don't know or refused
1   2   3   4

69. How do you feel about your inclusion in Jewish culture? Do you feel a lack of contact with Jewish culture (for example, with well-known Jewish politicians, artists, etc., absence of concerts, exhibitions, Jewish libraries), do you feel you have enough contact, or do you feel you have too much contact?

enough   too little   too much   don't know or refused
1   2   3   99

70. In your opinion, how important is it that Jewish culture be revived in your country today—not important or important?

not important   important   don't know or refused
1   2   99

71. Do the conditions exist for the real development of Jewish culture in your country?

yes   no   don't know or refused
1   2   99

72. Do you feel that it is better if Jews marry Jews, non-Jews or do you feel it's all the same?

Jews   non-Jews   it's all the same   don't know or refused
1   2   3   99

73. Do you bring your children up with Jewish traditions?

yes   no   have no children   don't know or refused
1   2   3   99

PART G [ATTITUDES TO EMIGRATION.]

74. Do you intend to emigrate from the country?

yes	no	don't know or refused
1	2	99

[Interviewer: Ask questions 75-82 only for those who answered "yes" on question 74.]

Why do you want to emigrate? I will read you a list of possible reasons that might be important for you. Please indicate the three most important reasons for you.

[Interviewer: specify "1" for every important reason and "99" for every reasons not chosen.]

_____ **75. to increase standard of living**

_____ **76. due to fear of political instability**

_____ **77. for the sake of children's future**

_____ **78. due to fear of antisemitism, pogroms**

_____ **79. due to fear of violence**

_____ **80. due to lack of belief in any improvement of the situation in the CIS**

_____ **81. in order to keep the family together**

82. To which country are you planning to emigrate?

Israel	USA	Canada	Australia	Germany
1	2	3	4	5

other	don't know or refused
6	99

[Interviewer: Ask questions 83-91 only for those who plan to emigrate to countries other than Israel.]

Why do you not want to emigrate to Israel? I will read you a list of possible reasons that might be important for you. Please indicate the three most important reasons for you.

[Interviewer: Specify "1" for every important reason and "99" for every reason not chosen.]

_____ 83. not enough good jobs there

_____ 84. fear of losing recent business

_____ 85. difficulties of living in a Jewish culture

_____ 86. fear of Arab-Israel conflict and the possibility of war

_____ 87. too few close friends and/or relatives there

_____ 88. the Hebrew language is too difficult to learn

_____ 89. I do not wish to leave Russia (Ukraine, Belarus)

_____ 90. old age, weak health

91. If you were assured of getting a job in Israel comparable to your current job, would you emigrate to Israel?

yes	no	don't know or refused
1	2	99

92. Do members of your immediate family or more distant relatives live in Israel?

yes	no	don't know or refused
1	2	99

93. Do members of your immediate family or more distant relatives live in the USA?

yes	no	don't know or refused
1	2	99

94. Do members of your immediate family or more distant relatives live in other Western countries?

yes	no	don't know or refused
1	2	99

95. And do you have friends living in Israel?

yes	no	don't know or refused
1	2	99

96. How about friends living in the USA?

yes   no   don't know or refused
1   2   99

97. Do you have friends living in other Western contries?

yes   no   don't know or refused
1   2   99

98. In your opinion, how many more Jews in your country will eventually emigrate--nearly all, a majority, about half, a minority, hardly any?

nearly all   a majority   about half   a minority   hardly any
1   2   3   4   5

don't know or refused
99

What connects you with the country you live in now? I'll read you a list of connections that might be important for you. Please indicate the three most important connections for you.

[Interviewer: Specify "1" for every connection and "99" for every connection not chosen.]

_____ 99. I have a good job.

_____ 100. I am accustomed to living in the country.

_____ 101. I hope to establish a business here.

_____ 102. I hope to increase my standard of living here.

_____ 103. I am unwilling to separate from my relatives.

_____ 104. I am unwilling to separate from my friends.

_____ 105. I hope for political stability in this country.

_____ 106. I am closely connected to this culture.

_____ 107. old age, weak health.

108. How do you feel about Israel?

[Interviewer: Read the options and ask the respondent to choose one.]

as if it is any other developed country	as if it is an eminent state	as if it is my historical motherland
1	2	3

I have no particular attitude towards Israel	other	don't know or refused
4	5	99

PART H [ANTISEMITISM.]

In your opinion, what does "antisemitism" mean?

[Interviewer: Do not read the options. Specify "1" for the first feature of antisemitism mentioned, "2" for the second, etc. Enter "99" for each option not selected.]

_____ **109. state policy of restrictions on Jews in some spheres of society and some places of work**

_____ **110. hostility towards Jews from ordinary people**

_____ **111. threats against Jews from nationalist organizations**

_____ **112. anti-Jewish articles in press**

_____ **113. envy of the Jews**

_____ **114. antisemitism doesn't exist, it is a fantasy of Jews themselves**

_____ **115. other**

116. Do you think that antisemitism exists in your country?

yes	no	don't know or refused
1	2	99

[Interviewer: Ask questions 117-124 for those who answered "yes" on question 116.]

What are the main manifestations of antisemitism in your country today?

[Interviewer: Do not read the list of options. Specify "1" for the first manifestation mentioned, "2" for the second, and so forth. Enter "99" for each option not selected.]

_____ 117. state policy of restrictions on Jews in some spheres of society   and some places of work

_____ 118. hostility towards Jews from ordinary people

_____ 119. threats against Jews from nationalist organizations

_____ 120. anti-Jewish articles in press

_____ 121. envy of the Jews

_____ 122. other

123. Have you personally suffered from manifestations of antisemitism?

yes	no	don't know or refused
1	2	99

[Interviewer: Ask questions 124-129 to respondents who answered "yes" to question 123.]

What were the main manifestations of antisemitism you suffered?

[Interviewer: Do not read the list of options. Specify "1" for the first manifestation mentioned, "2" for the next manifestation, and so forth. Enter "99" for each option not selected.]

_____ 124. state policy of restrictions on Jews in some spheres of society and some places of work

_____ 125. hostility towards Jews from ordinary people

_____ 126. threats against Jews from nationalist organizations

_____ 127. anti-Jewish articles in press

_____ 128. envy of the Jews

_____ 129. other

130. Do you fear the manifestations of antisemitism?

very much	not very much	not at all	don't know or refused
1	2	3	99

[Interviewer: Ask question 131 for those who answered "very much" or "not very much" on question 130.]

131. Is your fear of antisemitism now stronger, weaker or the same as compared to 6-7 years ago?

stronger	weaker	the same	don't know or refused
1	2	3	99

132. How likely do you think it is that pogroms will break out in your country in the near future--for sure, possible or impossible?

for sure	possible	impossible	don't know or refused
1	2	3	99

133. Thinking now about the situation over the past year, have you witnessed no antisemitism, a little antisemitism, or quite a lot of antisemitism at your place of work?

none	a little	quite a lot	don't know or refused	not applicable
1 2	3	99	9	

134. How about your neighbourhood?

none	a little	quite a lot	don't know or refused
1	2	3	99

135. How about in the mass media (press, radio and TV)?

none	a little	quite a lot	don't know or refused
1	2	3	99

136. And in state policy?

none	a little	quite a lot	don't know or refused
1	2	3	99

137. Thinking now about the next 1-2 years, do you expect you will witness less antisemitism, about the same, or more antisemitism at your place of work?

less	about the same	more	don't know or refused	not applicable
1	2	3	99	9

138. How about your neighbourhood?

less	about the same	more	don't know or refused	not applicable
1	2	3	99	9

139. How about in the mass media (press, radio and TV)?

less	about the same	more	don't know or refused	not applicable
1	2	3	99	9

140. And in state policy?

less	about the same	more	don't know or refused	not applicable
1	2	3	99	9

The view is becoming widespread that antisemitism exists in your country. In your opinion, who has an interest in spreading this view?

[Interviewer: Do not read the list of options. Specify "1" for the first option mentioned, "2" for the second option, and so forth. Enter "99" for each option not selected.]

_____ **141. political opposition in your country**

_____ **142. certain government officials in your country**

_____ **143. Jews inside your country**

_____ **144. Jewish organizations from former USSR**

_____ **145. Jewish organizations abroad**

_____ **146. Israel, USA and other Western contries**

_____ **147. nationalist parties and groups in your country**

_____ **148. other**

PART I [VALUES OF THE RESPONDENT.]

People have different values. For some people some things are important and for other people other things are important. What things are very important, or important, or not important for you?

[Interviewer: Indicate the degree of importance for each item below. Specify 1=very important, 2=important, 3=not important.]

_____ **149. success in business**

_____ **150. professional career**

_____ **151. good family**

_____ **152. good health**

_____ **153. respect from the people around me**

_____ **154. personal independence**

_____ **155. to be a leader**

_____ **156. to participate in making important decisions**

_____ **157. to help Russia (Ukraine, Belarus)**

_____ **158. to be in Israel**

159. If you could choose, in what era would you prefer to live--before 1917, during Lenin's rule, during Stalin's rule, during Khrushchev's rule, during Brezhnev's rule, during Gorbachev's rule, or during Yeltsin's rule?

before 1917	Lenin's rule	Stalin's rule	Khrushchev's	Brezhnev's
		rule	rule	
1	2	3	4	5

Gorbachev's rule	Yeltsin's rule	don't know or refused
6	7	99

160. If the current government had to resign, what sort of government would you prefer to rule the country next?

a government like the current one	a government headed by the military	a government headed by directors of large state plants
1	2	3

a government headed by entrepreneurs	Communist government
4	5

a religious government	a national-patriotic government	don't know or refused
6	7	99

161. Some people say that the country has reached its current crisis because Russian (Ukrainian, Belarusian) traditions and culture have been weakened by Western influence. Other people say that the country needs even more Western influence in order to solve its problems. Do you think that Western influence in your country now is too much, enough or not enough?

too much	enough	not enough	don't know or refused
1	2	3	99

162. What do you think the political system of your country is likely to be in 1-2 years—freer, less free or the same?

freer	less free	the same	don't know or refused
1	2	3	99

163. Do you have confidence in your own future?

yes	no	don't know or refused
1	2	99

PART J [REMARKS ABOUT INTERVIEW. TO BE COMPLETED BY THE INTERVIEWER AFTER THE INTERVIEW HAS BEEN COMPLETED AND OUTSIDE OF THE RESPONDENT'S HOUSEHOLD.]

164. How many minutes did the interview take?_____

165. Indicate on a scale of 1 to 5 how open or closed the respondent seemed to feel in answering the questions.

very open				very closed	don'tknow or refused
1	2	3	4	5	99

In your opinion, which question(s), if any, were dificult for the respondent to understand? You may indicate up to twelve questions below. Please insert "99" in any positions left blank.

166._____   167._____   168._____   169._____   170._____

171._____   172._____   173._____   174._____   175._____

176._____   177._____

178. In how many households did you try to secure a respondent before succeeding in securing this one? _____

Answer the following questions only if you could not interview the randomly selected respondent from this household. Obtain the information from another household member.

179. What was the sex of the respondent whom you could not interview?

male	female	don't know or refused
1	2	99

180. What was the age of the respondent whom you could not interview?

_____ years   99 don't know or refused

181. What level of schooling did the respondent whom you could not interview complete?

less than elementary school	elementary school (grades 7-8)	middle school (grades 9-11)	technical-professional school	teknikum
1	2	3	4	5

at least some university	Ph.D.	Doctor of Science (Full Professor)		don't know or refused
6	7	8		99

Sources Cited

Alexander, Zvi, "Jewish emigration from the USSR in 1980", *Soviet Jewish Affairs*, vol. 11, no. 2, 1981, 3-21

Altshuler, Mordechai, "The Jewish Community in the Soviet Union: A Sociodemographic Analysis" (Jerusalem: Magnes Press, Hebrew University of Jerusalem, 1979) (in Hebrew)

_____ "Jews and Russians-1991", "The Jews in the Soviet Union" (in Hebrew), vol. 15, 1992, 31-43

_____ "Socio-demographic profile of Moscow Jews", *Jews and Jewish Topics in the Soviet Union and Eastern Europe*, 3 (16), 1991, 24-40

_____ *Soviet Jewry since the Second World War: Population and Social Structure* (New York: Greenwood, 1987)

Antisemitism World Report 1992 (London: Institute of Jewish Affairs, 1992)

Antisemitism World Report 1993 (London: Institute of Jewish Affairs, 1993)

Basok, Tanya and Robert J. Brym, "Soviet-Jewish emigration and resettlement in the 1990s: An overview" in Tanya Basok and Robert J. Brym (eds.), *Soviet-Jewish Emigration and Resettlement in the 1990s* (Toronto: York Lanes Press, York University, 1991), xi-xxii

Benifand, Alexander, "Jewish emigration from the USSR in the 1990s" in Tanya Basok and Robert J. Brym (eds.), *Soviet-Jewish Emigration and Resettlement in the 1990s* (Toronto: York Lanes Press, York University, 1991), 39-50

Bertsch, Gary, "US-Soviet trade: The question of leverage", *Survey,* vol. 25, no. 2, 1980, 66-80

Bestuzhev-Lada, Igor, "Social problems of the Soviet way of life", *Novy mir,* no. 7, 1976, 208-21

Beyer, Gregg A., "The evolving United States response to Soviet-Jewish emigration" in Tanya Basok and Robert J. Brym (eds.), *Soviet-Jewish Emigration and Resettlement in the 1990s* (Toronto: York Lanes Press, York University, 1991), 105-39

132

Bodemann, Michal, "A renaissance of Germany Jewry?", paper presented at a conference on The Reemergence of Jewish Culture in Germany (University of Toronto, 6-7 May 1993)

Bogoraz, Larisa, "Do I feel I belong to the Jewish people?" in Aleksandr Voronel, Viktor Yakhot and Moshe Decter (eds.), *I am a Jew: Essays on Jewish Identity in the Soviet Union* (New York: Academic Committee on Soviet Jewry and Anti-Defamation League of B'nai B'rith, 1973), 60-4

Brodbar-Nemzer, Jay *et al.,* "An overview of the Canadian Jewish community" in Robert J. Brym, William Shaffir and Morton Weinfeld (eds.), *The Jews in Canada* (Toronto: Oxford University Press, 1993), 39-71

Bromley, J. *et al., Present-Day Ethnic Processes in the USSR* (Moscow: Progress Publishers 1982 [1977])

Brym, Robert J., "The changing rate of Jewish emigration from the USSR: Some lessons from the 1970s", *Soviet Jewish Affairs*, vol. 15, no. 2, 1985, 23-35

_____ "From 'The Soviet people' to the refugee crisis in Russia" in Rozalina Ryvkina and Rostislav Turovskiy, *The Refugee Crisis in Russia*, R. Brym, ed., P. Patchet-Golubev, trans. (Toronto: York Lanes Press, 1993), 1-7

_____ "The emigration potential of Czechoslovakia, Hungary, Lithuania, Poland and Russia: Recent survey results", *International Sociology,* vol. 7, no. 4, 1992, 387-95

_____ "*Perestroyka*, public opinion, and *Pamyat*", *Soviet Jewish Affairs,* vol. 19, no. 3, 1989, 23-32

_____ "Sociology, *perestroika*, and Soviet society", *Canadian Journal of Sociology*, vol. 15, no. 2, 1990, 207-15

_____ "Soviet-Jewish emigration: A statistical test of two theories", *Soviet Jewish Affairs,* vol. 18, no. 3, 1988, 15-23

_____ and Andrei Degtyarev, "Anti-Semitism in Moscow: Results of an October 1992 survey", *Slavic Review*, vol. 52, no. 1, 1993, 1-12

_____ and Andrei Degtyarev, "Who wants to leave Moscow for the West? Results of an October 1992 survey," *Refuge,* vol. 13, no. 2, 1993, 24-5

_____ and Rhonda L. Lenton, "The distribution of antisemitism in Canada in 1984", *Canadian Journal of Sociology*, vol. 16, no. 4, 1991, 411-18

Bútorová, Zora and Martin Bútora, "Wariness towards Jews as an expression of post-Communist panic: The case of Slovakia", *Czechoslovak Sociological Review*, Special Issue, no. 28, 1992, 92-106

Chernenko, I. V. and M. M. Zakhvatkin, "The fascism-socialism dichotomy from the point of view of catastrophe theory", *Rossiysky monitor: Arkhiv sovremennoy politiki*, no. 1, 1992, 92-3

Cohen, Roberta, "Israel's problematic absorption of Soviet Jews" in Tanya Basok and Robert J. Brym (eds.), *Soviet-Jewish Emigration and Resettlement in the 1990s* (Toronto: York Lanes Press, York University, 1991), 67-89

Cohen, Steven M., *American Modernity and Jewish Identity* (New York and London: Tavistock, 1983)

Cole, John P. and Igor V. Filatotchev, "Some observations on migration within and from the former USSR in the 1990s", *Post-Soviet Geography*, vol. 33, no. 7, 1992, 432-53

"Cutback", *Pravda*, 4 March 1988

DellaPergolla, Sergio, "The demographic context of the Soviet aliya", *Jews and Jewish Topics in the Soviet Union and Eastern Europe*, (16, 3), 1991, 41-56

Dunn, John F., "Hard times in Russia foster conspiracy theories", Radio Free Europe/ Radio Liberty Special Report, 23 September 1992

Erlanger, Steven, "As Ukraine loses Jews, the Jews lose a tradition", *The New York Times*, 27 August 1992

Feshbach, Murray, "The Soviet Union: Population trends and dilemmas", *Population Bulletin*, vol. 37, no. 3, 1982, 1-45

"5 million Jews in CIS", *Canadian Jewish News*, 29 April 1993

Frankel, Jonathan, "The Soviet regime and anti-Zionism: An analysis" in Yaacov Ro'i and Avi Beker, (eds.), *Jewish Culture and Identity in the Soviet Union* (New York and London: New York University Press, 1991), 310-54

Freedman, Robert O., "Soviet Jewry as a factor in Soviet-Israeli relations" in Robert O. Freedman (ed.), *Soviet Jewry in the 1980s: The Politics of Anti-Semitism and Emigration and the Dynamics of Resettlement* (Durham NC: Duke University Press, 1989), 61-96

_____ "Soviet Jewry and Soviet-American relations" in Robert O. Freedman (ed.), *Soviet Jewry in the Decisive Decade, 1971-80* (Durham, NC: Duke University Press, 1984), 38-67

Friedgut, Theodore, "Soviet Jewry: The silent majority", *Soviet Jewish Affairs*, vol. 10, no. 2, 1980, 3-19

_____ "Soviet anti-Zionism and antisemitism--Another cycle", *Soviet Jewish Affairs*, vol. 14, no. 1, 1984, 3-22

Gibson, James L. and Raymond M. Duch, "Anti-semitic attitudes of the mass public: Estimates and explanations based on a survey of the Moscow oblast", *Public Opinion Quarterly,* no. 56, 1992, 1-28

Gilbert, Martin *Churchill: A Life* (London: Minerva, 1991)

Gilboa, Yehoshua A., *The Black Years of Soviet Jewry, 1939-1953*, Yosef Shachter and Dov Ben-Abba, trans. (Boston: Little, Brown, 1971)

Gitelman, Zvi, "The evolution of Jewish culture and identity in the Soviet Union" in Yaacov Ro'i and Avi Beker (eds.), *Jewish Culture and Identity in the Soviet Union* (New York and London: New York University Press, 1991), 3-24

_____ "Glasnost, perestroika and antisemitism", *Foreign Affairs*, vol. 70, no. 2, 1991, 141-59

_____ *Jewish Nationality and Soviet Politics: The Jewish Sections of the CPSU, 1917-1930* (Princeton NJ: Princeton University Press, 1972)

_____ "Recent demographic and migratory trends among Soviet Jews: Implications for policy", *Post-Soviet Geography*, vol. 33, no. 3, 1992, 139-45

_____ "Soviet Jewish emigrants: Why are they choosing America?", *Soviet Jewish Affairs*, vol. 7, no. 1, 1977, 31-46

Goldman, Marshall I., "Soviet-American trade and Soviet Jewish emigration: Should a policy change be made by the American Jewish community?" in Robert O. Freedman (ed.), *Soviet Jewry in the 1980s: The Politics of Anti-Semitism and Emigration and the Dynamics of Resettlement* (Durham NC: Duke University Press, 1989), 141-59

Government of Israel, "The State Budget for 1993: Submitted to the Thirteenth Knesset" (Jerusalem: Government Printer, 1992) (in Hebrew)

Gudkov, Lev D. and Alex G. Levinson, *Attitudes Toward Jews in the Soviet Union: Public Opinion in Ten Republics* (New York: The American Jewish Committee, 1992)

_____ "Attitudes towards Jews", *Sotsiologicheskiye issledovaniya,* no. 12, 1992, 108-11

Havel, Václav, "The post-Communist nightmare", *The New York Review of Books*, 27 May 1993

Hechter, Michael, "Group formation and the cultural division of labor", *American Journal of Sociology*, no. 84, 1978, 293-318

Heitman, Sidney, "Jewish emigration from the former USSR in 1992", unpublished paper (Fort Collins CO: 1993)

_____ "Jews in the 1989 USSR census", *Soviet Jewish Affairs*, vol. 20, no. 1, 1990, 23-30

Hertzberg, Arthur, "Is anti-Semitism dying out?", *The New York Review of Books*, 24 June 1993

"Iadov, V. *et al.*, "The sociopolitical situation in Russia in mid-February 1992", *Sociological Research*, vol. 32, no. 2, 1993, 6-32

Immigration data-1991" in "The Jews in the Soviet Union", vol. 15, 1992, 188-91

Karklins, Rasma, *Ethnic Relations in the USSR: The Perspective from Below* (London: Unwin Hyman, 1986)

_____ "Nationality policy and ethnic relations in the USSR" in James R. Millar (ed.), *Politics, Work, and Daily Life in the USSR: A Survey of Former Soviet Citizens* (Cambridge UK: Cambridge University Press, 1987), 305-31

Koltsov, V. B. and V. A. Mansurov, "Political ideologies during the period of *perestroyka*", *Sotsiologicheskiye issledovaniya*, no. 10, 1991, 22-35

Komozin, A., (ed.), *Monitoring: The 1993 Russian Citizens' Opinion Poll Results* (Moscow: Institute of Sociology, Russian Academy of Sciences, 1993)

Kostakov, Vladimir G., "Employment: deficit or surplus?", *Kommunist*, no. 2, 1987, 78-89

"Kosygin on reunion of families and national equality (1966)" in Benjamin Pinkus (ed.), *The Soviet Government and the Jews 1948-1967* (Cambridge UK: Cambridge University Press, 1984), 77-8

Lambert, Ronald D. and James E. Curtis "*Québécois* and English Canadian opposition to racial and religious intermarriage, 1968-1983", *Canadian Ethnic Studies*, vol. 16, no. 2, 1984, 30-46

Lenton, Rhonda L., "Home versus career: Attitudes towards women's work among Russian women and men, 1992", *Canadian Journal of Sociology*, vol. 18, no. 3, 1993, 325-31

Lieberson, Stanley and Mary Waters, "Ethnic groups in flux: The changing ethnic responses of American whites", *Annals of the American Academy of Social and Political Science*, no. 487, 1986, 79-91

Lowenthal, Richard, "East-West *détente* and the future of Soviet Jewry", *Soviet Jewish Affairs*, vol. 3, no. 1, 1973, 20-5

Margolina, Sonja, *Das Ende der Lügen: Rußland und die Juden im 20. Jahrhundert* (Berlin: Siedler Verlag, 1992)

Marnie, Sheila, "How prepared is Russia for mass unemployment?", Radio Free Europe/Radio Liberty Special Report, 11 November 1992

"Meetings between representatives of the French Socialist Party and Soviet leaders (1956)" in Benjamin Pinkus (ed.), *The Soviet Government and the Jews 1948-1967* (Cambridge UK: Cambridge University Press, 1984), 55-8

"Miscellaneous reports", *Chronicle of Current Events*, no. 52, 1980 [1979], 123-33

Morozova, G. F., "Refugees and emigrants", *Sociological Research*, vol. 32, no. 2, 1993, 86-96

Moscow Helsinki Monitoring Group, *Discrimination Against Jews Enrolling at Moscow State University, 1979*, Document 112 (n.p.: 5 November 1979, mimeograph)

Motyl, Alexander J., *Will the Non-Russians Rebel? State, Ethnicity, and Stability in the USSR* (Ithaca and London: Cornell University Press, 1987)

Nationalities Papers, Special Issue on *Pamyat*, vol. 19, no. 2, 1991

Nezer, Zvi, "Jewish emigration from the USSR in 1981-82", *Soviet Jewish Affairs*, vol. 12, no. 3, 1982, 3-17

"One-year limit on US refugee status for ex-USSR", *Monitor: Digest of News and Analysis from Soviet Successor States,* vol. 4, no. 25, 30 July/6 August 1993

Orlova, Irena, "A sketch of the migration and refugee situation in Russia", *Refuge,* vol. 13, no. 2, 1993, 19-22

Pipes, Richard, "The Soviet Union adrift", *Foreign Affairs*, vol. 70, no. 1, 1991, 70-87

_____ "Soviet relations with the USA", Lukasz Hirszowicz (ed.), *Proceedings of the Experts' Conference on Soviet Jewry Today: London, 4-6 January 1983* (London: Institute of Jewish Affairs, 1985), 107-12

Popov, Nikolai, "Political views of the Russian public", *The International Journal of Public Opinion Research*, vol. 4, no. 4, 1992, 321-34

_____ Roussina Volkova and Vadim Sazonov, "Unemployment in Science: Executive Summary" (Moscow: VTsIOM, 1991)

Reddaway, Peter, "Policy towards dissent since Khrushchev" in T. H. Rigby, Archie Brown and Peter Reddaway (eds.), *Authority, Power and Policy in the USSR: Essays Dedicated to Leonard Shapiro* (London: Macmillan: 1980), 158-92

Ribakovsky, L. L. and N. V. Tarasova, "Migration processes in the USSR: New phenomena", *Sotsiologicheskiye issledovaniya*, no. 7, 1990, 32-41

Rosenfield, Geraldine, "The polls: Attitudes toward American Jews", *Public Opinion Quarterly*, no. 46, 1982, 431-43

Rukavishnikov, V. O. *et al.*, "Social tension: Diagnosis and prognosis", *Sociological Research*, vol. 32, no. 2, 1993, 33-65

Ryansky, Felix, "Jews and Cossacks in the Jewish Autonomous Region", *Refuge*, vol. 12, no. 4, 1992, 19-21

Ryvkina, Rozalina, "Value conflicts of Russian Jews and their social types", unpublished paper (Moscow 1992)

_____ "From civic courage to scientific demonstration", *Soviet Sociology*, vol. 28, no. 5, 1989, 7-23

Salitan, Laurie P., *Politics and Nationality in Contemporary Soviet-Jewish Emigration, 1968-89* (New York: St. Martin's, 1992)

Sartre, Jean-Paul *Anti-Semite and Jew*, trans. George J. Becker (New York: Schocken, 1965 [1948])

Schwarz, Solomon M., *The Jews in the Soviet Union* (Syracuse NY: Syracuse University Press, 1951)

Sedov, L. A., "Yeltsin's rating", *Ekonomicheskiye i sotsialnye peremeny: Monitoring obshchestvennogo mneniya*, Informatsionny byulleten, Intertsentr VTsIOM (Moscow: Aspekt Press, 1993), 14-15

Sharansky, Natan, "The greatest exodus", *The New York Times Magazine*, 2 February 1992

Shevchenko, Arkady N., *Breaking with Moscow* (New York: Alfred A. Knopf, 1985)

"The socioeconomic situation of the Russian Federation, January-March 1993", *Ekonomichesky obzor*, no. 4, Goskomstat Rossii (Moscow: Respublikansky informatsionno-izdatelsky tsentr, 1993)

"Soviet anti-Semitism said to be ceasing", *Canadian Jewish News*, 20 August 1987

Starovoitova, Galina, "Weimar Russia?", *Journal of Democracy*, vol. 4, no. 3, 1993, 106-9

"Surplus loan guarantees", *Canadian Jewish News*, 17 June 1993

Swafford, Michael, "Sociological aspects of survey research in the Commonwealth of Independent States", *International Journal of Public Opinion Research*, vol. 4, no. 4, 1992, 346-57

Tolts, Mark, "Jewish marriages in the USSR: A demographic analysis", *East European Jewish Affairs*, vol. 22, no. 2, 1993, 3-19

Tsigelman, Ludmilla, "The impact of ideological changes in the USSR on different generations of the Soviet Jewish intelligentsia" in Yaacov Ro'i and Avi Beker (eds.), *Jewish Culture and Identity in the Soviet Union* (New York and London: New York University Press, 1991), 42-72

Zaslavskaya, Tatyana, "*Perestroyka* and sociology", *Pravda*, 6 February 1987

Zaslavsky, Victor and Robert J. Brym, *Soviet-Jewish Emigration and Soviet Nationality Policy* (London: Macmillan, 1983)

Zotov, Vladimir, "The Chechen problem as seen by Muscovites", *Moskovsky komsomolets*, 12 January 1993

Name Index

Subject Index